WATERCOLOUR PAINTING

Easy Solutions to Colour Painting

WATERCOLOUR PAINTING

Easy Solutions to Colour Painting

M. Stephen Doherty

Quantum
Books

A QUANTUM BOOK

Published by
Quantum Publishing Ltd
6 Blundell Street
London N7 9BH

Copyright © MCMXCVIII
Rockport Publishers, Inc

This edition printed 2003

All rights reserved.
This book is protected by copyright. No part of it may be reproduced, stored in a retrieval system, or transmitted in any form or by any means, without the prior permission in writing of the Publisher, nor be otherwise circulated in any form of binding or cover other than that in which it is published and without a similar condition including this condition being imposed on the subsequent publisher.

ISBN 1-86160-643-5

QUMESCM

Printed in China by
Midas Printing Limited

Additional images credited as follows:

MAY FLOWERS (Detail) Deborah L. Chabrian, 28 cm x 33 cm (11" x 13"), PAGE 2

MORNING SHOPPERS, DINAN Robert A.Wade, 28 cm x 20 cm (11" x 8"), PAGE 5

VENICE I Jean Grastorf, 71 cm x 51 cm (28" x 20"), PAGE 6

FRESH EGGS Sharon Weilbaecher, 99 cm x 71 cm (39" x 28"), PAGE 10

Acknowledgments

My thanks first go to the artists who have generously provided the information and photographs that make this book valuable.

Next, I want to acknowledge the creative contributions of the editors, designers and marketing staff at Rockport Publishers.

To my parents, Chic and Dot Doherty, I express my appreciation for a lifetime of support and encouragement.

Finally, I extend my heartfelt thanks to my wife, Sara and our children, Clare and Michael.

CONTENTS

INTRODUCTION

SECTION 1 – Colour Mixing for Still Lifes
14

Building on Harmonious Colours – *Daryl Bryant*
18

Balancing Related Colours – *Deborah L, Chabrian*
26

Shaping Objects with Colour – *Denise Lisiecki*
34

SECTION II – Colour Mixing for Florals
42

Maximizing Colour Mixtures – *Susan Headley Van Campen*
46

Getting Colours to Work Together – Mary *Weinstein*
54

Pouring Luminous Washes – Jean *Grastorf*
62

SECTION III ~ Colour Mixing for Landscapes
70

Emphasizing Colour Shapes ~ *Skip Lawrence*
74

Starting with Tonal Washes ~ *Robert A. Wade*
82

Controlling Colour Washes ~ *Denise Lisiecki*
90

SECTION IV ~ Colour Mixing for Wildlife
98

Detailing with Thin Washes ~ *Jenny Pearse*
102

Floating Colours on to Damp Paper ~ *Sharon Weilbaecher*
110

Mixing Intense Bright Colours ~ *Colleen Newport Stevens*
118

COLOUR IN THE STUDIO 126

Contributors 136

Index 142

About the Author 144

INTRODUCTION
Colour Choices in the Studio

For those who have never tried it, watercolour seems like an easy medium to master. After all, the only materials needed are a sheet of paper, a brush and a few tubes of paint; and the only technique to learn is stirring water into paint. But after beginners make a few paintings with garish green trees, dark black rocks, muddy brown water and ominous grey skies, they realize there is more to handling watercolour than they ever imagined.

The most important lesson novices must learn is that the successful use of watercolour depends on the proper selection and mixture of tube colours. The decision of what colours to choose and how to mix them makes the difference between a glowing, vibrant painting and a dull, muddy mess!

The purpose of this book is to provide users with some practical tips on choosing and mixing tube colours. The twelve artists who have contributed to this book offer an enormous amount of information about colour choices and colour mixtures that can be helpful to any watercolourist, beginner or advanced. Each artist details the selection of pigments, the combinations of colours on their palettes and on the surface of their paintings and the steps they take to avoid problems.

You'll find that the artists each have very different approaches to colour – some of which seem to conflict with others. Skip Lawrence extols the virtues of opaque colours such as cerulean blue and yellow ochre, while Jean Grastorf cautions against using anything but transparent, staining colours like phthalo blue and Hansa yellow deep. Both artists use colour mixtures that work beautifully with their respective painting techniques. Lawrence seeks colours that sink into the paper and create soft, rich landscape forms; Grastorf features staining colours that she can pour in layers to establish glowing light in a floral arrangement.

non-staining watercolours

As you read each chapter and understand why the artists create their own colour mixtures, you'll gain an understanding of watercolour paints that will help you formulate your own creative approach to the medium. You may decide to copy Lawrence's palette, or you may prefer to combine some of his colours with ones Grastorf recommends. As long as you are in control of the medium and are achieving the results you want, you're making the correct colour mixtures for your paintings.

As a way of introducing the options available to you, I've painted two columns of colours that seem almost exactly alike. I mixed two separate sets of colours to get the same orange, green, brown and purple. You might conclude, then, that any combination of colours gives the same results. But if you look at the columns to the left and right of the matching columns, you'll see that when I painted over the original colour mixtures or dampened the original squares the results were quite different.

The reason for the differing results is that I painted one column with mixtures of pigments that don't stain the fibres of the paper and the adjacent column with all staining colours. The non-staining colours quickly mixed with the layers of paint applied over them and easily lifted off the paper when they were dampened. The staining colours, on the other hand, didn't budge. So the staining properties of colours are important to the way they mix.

You'll see in the colour workshop sections that the featured artists also concern themselves with complementary colours, synthetic and organic pigments, particulating colours, harmonious tones and colour temperatures. These are just a few of the characteristics you'll want to know about as you choose your palette.

You may be concerned that all this technical information will get in the way of enjoying the creative potential of the medium. It's true that you'll need to digest a lot of material at first. But as you work with colours, you'll get to know them so well that you'll soon have an instinctive understanding of how to mix them. You'll come to have your favourite tube colours, as each of the featured artists does, and you'll know just how to combine them to paint that hybrid rose, copper kettle or distant mountain.

watercolours that stain the fibres of the paper

SUMMER DESSERT *Deborah L. Chabrian*, 27.9 cm x 33 cm (11" X 13")

Colour

Mixing

for

Still Lifes

Still-life painting is a process of working with the subtle relationships between the shapes of objects, the textures and surfaces that identify them and the colours that bring them together. It involves selecting one piece because it is tall and thin, another because it has a shiny surface and a third because it can be laid between to connect the two objects. And during the painting process, still-life painting means repeating colours, adjusting values and balancing intense pigments with soft ones. If the painter includes a bright red bottle on the left side of the picture, he or she needs to work some of that same red pigment into the wooden box on the right. Otherwise, the painting will seem awkward and unbalanced.

The three artists featured in this section explain how they achieve those subtle relationships by controlling the mixtures of colours they select for their palettes. All three work directly from observations of pears, apples, chequered fabrics and other objects that are right in front of them. They challenge themselves to use what they see – the exact colours, shapes and arrangements – while interpreting their observations in very personal ways. That is, they make note of the real colours in nature but adjust them in an individual manner.

Daryl Bryant mixes a lot of water with her tube colours and lets each colour flow into the others on the watercolour paper. She shows you how she maintains the soft edges of the pears, apples and cloth during the early stages of the painting process, and then adds hard edges towards the end. That com-bination of hard and soft edges helps to unify the picture, blend the colours and create an appealing watercolour.

Deborah L. Chabrian also uses techniques that lend harmony to the colours in her still life, but she uses different paints and paper from Bryant. She seals and tones her smooth paper with one colour (in the case of her demonstration painting, yellow ochre), which then mixes with all the other layers of paint. This process allows her to distinguish objects with the slightest shifts towards red, orange, blue or green.

Denise Lisiecki is much less direct in mixing and applying colours, but she too aims for balance and harmony between pigments. She first makes careful studies of the way each pigment performs before applying it to the watercolour paper. This approach helps her decide how to use both complementary and analogous colours to capture the vitality and richness of what she observes.

SUN-BLEACHED SHELL *Daryl Bryant*, 55.9 cm x 38.1 cm (22" x 15")

Building on Harmonious Colours

"I love quick, gestural strokes of transparent colour that suggest the appearance of real objects, people and places. But the only way to know all those active marks will come together in a successful painting is to plan ahead."

– Daryl Bryant

Daryl Bryant applies strokes of fluid colour on to a sheet of watercolour paper already made damp by preliminary washes of soft, harmonious colours. The colours blend and remain glowingly transparent. The artist mixes most of the colours on the paper itself to keep them from becoming muddy. This technique allows her to incorporate almost any colour – opaque or transparent – but she limits herself to colours that arc close to each other on the colour wheel or are blended from the same limited number of tube colours.

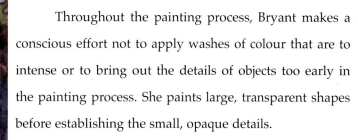

Throughout the painting process, Bryant makes a conscious effort not to apply washes of colour that are to intense or to bring out the details of objects too early in the painting process. She paints large, transparent shapes before establishing the small, opaque details.

Bryant completes her paintings in one sitting so that the colours won't completely dry into the fibres of the watercolour paper until she is satisfied with the picture. Until that point, she is able to manipulate the colours, values and edges of the painting. "I set aside the time I need and turn the answering machine on so I can devote my full attention to the painting until it is finished", she explains. "If I look at the picture a couple of days later and find it needs a lot of adjustments, I'm likely to just toss it out and start a new painting. An over-worked watercolour loses the vibrancy of the colours and the vitality of the brush strokes."

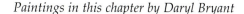

Paintings in this chapter by Daryl Bryant

(Opposite) CUP OF TEA 55.9 cm x 38.1 cm (22" x 15")
(Top) BEAN JUG 38.1 cm x 55.9 cm (15" x 22")
(Centre) SUN-BLEACHED SHELL 55.9 cm x 38.1 cm (22" x 15")
(Bottom) CHINESE VASE 38.1 cm x 55.9 cm (15" x 22")

Getting Started

Palette

Bryant avoids earth colours because they look chalky when they become thick. When she finds herself repeating the same colours, she changes her palette or technique for applying colour. Likewise, she switches from horizontal to vertical formats so each painting has its own problems and opportunities.

Favourites: Manganese blue and permanent rose.

Brushes

Bryant uses large flat brushes for the initial washes of colour and large round brushes for the rest of the painting. Towards the end of the process, she uses smaller round brushes, but even these are relatively large.

Favourites: 3 cm (1½") flat brush mode from natural and synthetic hairs; round brushes in sizes no. 18 and no. 20.

Surface

Bryant uses Winsor & Newton paper. She dampens the paper, stretches it on Gatorboard, or foam board covered with contact paper, and staples the two together. She applies fluid mixtures of paint that saturate the paper. This dampness helps her maintain soft edges and saturated colours until later in the process.

Favourite: Winsor & Newton paper.

Bryant's studio is in a Craftsman-style building that was originally constructed as a private residence and was subsequently divided into small offices. Despite the limited space, she appreciates the privacy and historic setting.

Bryant places the board holding the watercolour paper in a painting easel so she can work standing up, or props it against a drawing horse so she can sit and look at the developing image. She keeps the windows covered to prevent sunlight from changing the illumination on the painting surface. Artificial lights are focused on her subjects and paper.

To determine the composition and proportions of a full-scale watercolour, Bryant makes thumbnail sketches of her subjects. Along with the two or three compositional sketches, she makes notations about the various colours she might use in creating a painting. All of that information helps her make a full-scale, freehand pencil drawing on the stretched watercolour paper.

The first washes of colour Bryant applies to the paper are light in value, allowing her to establish a 'road map' for the rest of the painting. Those fluid washes also dampen the surface so that subsequent applications of colour are intense and soft-edged. As she paints layers of more intense colours, Bryant works around the entire picture so one area doesn't dominate the others.

Building on Harmonious Colours

Bryant makes small watercolour sketches and colour studies in her sketchbook to evaluate the layout, compositional possibilities and colours. She considers both a vertical and a horizontal format for the painting, and makes a grey-and-white value sketch to check the arrangement of values.

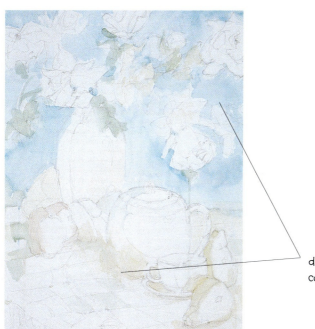

diluted colour washes

The artist makes a larger drawing on the stretched 140-lb cold-pressed watercolour paper and applies the first diluted washes of harmonious colour with 3 cm (1¼") and 5 cm (2") flat brushes. She uses Antwerp blue for the background, brightens the light-struck areas of the vase with Winsor violet and a touch of permanent rose and washes Hooker's green dark into the area of the tablecloth.

ADVICE FROM THE ARTIST

Think of the painting process as a search for the right colours and values. Try to focus on the planes of colour shapes made up of dark, light and middle values rather than, spaces that need to be filled in.

Daryl Bryant

3 ▶

Continuing to develop the basic shapes, Bryant uses Winsor violet, Antwerp blue and permanent rose for the vase. She pulls some of the Antwerp blue from the background to darken the shadowed side of the vase. She moves paint from one area to another to make colour connections, and lightly touches the hard edges with a brush dipped in water to soften those edges.

◀ 4

Continuing to use large flat and round brushes, Bryant applies cadmium red to the apples, then drops in some Winsor yellow, cadmium orange and manganese blue. She establishes the shade of the pears with burnt sienna and yellow ochre; pulls together the mass of leaves with Winsor yellow, cobalt green and ultramarine blue; and adds permanent rose and alizarin crimson for warmth and variation.

5

Bryant applies a wash of permanent rose to intensify the vase colour while keeping a bright tone and then adds a mix of Winsor violet and cobalt blue to the wet surface. She works the background shadow with Antwerp blue and Winsor violet, pulling some of the Antwerp blue into the tablecloth to darken its value.

 6

Bryant now uses less water to dissolve the paint so she can 'punch up' the colour with stronger applications of pigment. She also uses slightly smaller brushes and pays more attention to detail as she shapes the teapot and cup. She paints a minimal amount of calligraphy on those two objects, using ultramarine blue, and darkens the leaves with a mixture of ultramarine blue, Hooker's green and Winsor yellow.

ADVICE FROM THE ARTIST

Use thin mixtures of heavy colours like Hooker's green dark, yellow ochre and cerulean blue; and avoid letting the earth colours (burnt sienna) get too thick.

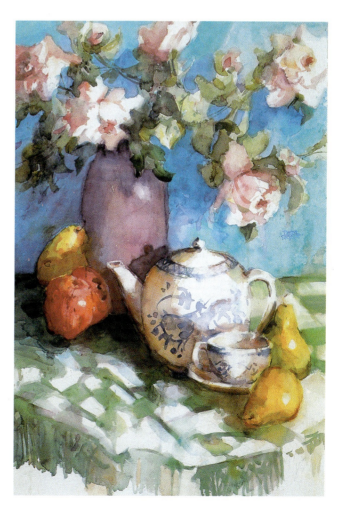

7

The artist pulls the green into the foreground to show the fringed edge of the chequered cloth and darkens the shadows on the left side. She also darkens the blue background to help the flowers stand out more distinctly.

BUILDING ON HARMONIOUS COLOURS

Colour Mixing Workshop

Value Study

A quickly painted value study like this one helps Bryant determine how she will use the colours in the painting.

Staining Colours

Bryant begins her demonstration using Antwerp blue, Winsor violet with a touch of permanent rose and Hooker's green dark – three intense, staining colours that work well together because they are kept transparent and damp.

Antwerp blue

Winsor violet & permanent rose

Hooker's green dark

One of the controlling ingredients in any colour mixture is the water added to the pigments while they are on the palette or when they are stroked across the damp watercolour paper. The more water added to the tube colours, the more transparent they become; and the more moisture. On the paper's surface, the more deeply the colours will sink into the fibres and become soft. Conversely, when very little water is mixed on the palette or when the paint is applied to bone – dry paper, the colours will become dense and either translucent or completely opaque.

> *The more water added to the tube colours, the more transparent they become.*

Daryl Bryant demonstrates how transparent, opaque and staining colours can all be made light, soft and luminous by

(Above) BRASS POT 28 cm x 38.1 cm (11" x 15")
(Opposite) RUSSIAN SHAWL 55.9 cm x 38.1 cm (22" x 15")

keeping them moist through the painting process. That technique allows her to use a wider range of colour mixtures than would be possible with drier applications of paint.

Note that Bryant does not thin her paints so much that the colours become faint and wispy. She uses lots of paint, stirs it thoroughly in the water and applies it to the damp paper with a well-charged brush. The resulting shapes are soft-edged and transparent, but they are not timid.

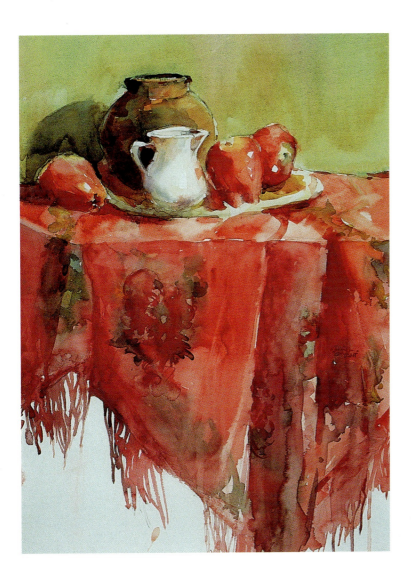

Thicker Mixtures of Colours

The artist is able to continue using thicker mixtures of the same three colours because the paper is wet enough for the pigments to blend together and sink into the fibres.

Layering over Dried Paint

Here, Bryant paints the Winsor violet after the Antwerp blue and Winsor violet have dried. Notice that instead of blending into a harmonious colour, the combination yields rather dark, grey colours.

Blending Harmonious Colours

Bryant achieves wonderful effects by blending harmonious colours while they are still wet. She paints the apple by first applying cadmium red and then dropping in Winsor yellow, cadmium orange and manganese blue.

BUILDING ON HARMONIOUS COLOURS

Balancing Related Colours

*"I don't need paints from all over the palette to get clear distinctions
between colours in the paintings I do on hot-pressed paper.
In fact, when I work within a limited range of harmonious tones,
the slightest shifts in colour become much more apparent."*

– **Deborah L. Chabrian**

One of the most critical aspects of Deborah L. Chabrian's technique is working with a limited numbers of colours, especially muted reds, blues and ochres. She mixes those harmonious tones by allowing four or five colours to blend together on her palette, so that each new combination begins with the colours already in use. This method is a bit like using some starter bread dough saved from one batch to make the next loaf.

With her colours confined to a limited range of intermixed pigments, Chabrian is able to maximize the subtle differences between those colours. A slight shift towards red, blue or yellow becomes more obvious than if she were to use completely separate tube colours for every shape within her picture.

Another important component is the smooth paper on which Chabrian paints. The polished surface of hot-pressed paper absorbs paint slowly, so particles of pigment separate and cling to the edges of shapes as they dry. The dried pigment gives the open areas a mottled look and forms a thin line around the painted shapes. Furthermore, because so much of the pigment sits on the surface of the paper, the artist can more easily soften edges and lighten values than she could on cold-pressed or rough paper. She can enhance these characteristics of the paper by mixing colours with Chinese white to make them opaque and to seal the paper. The colours then take on a milky tinted look.

Paintings in this chapter by Deborah L. Chabrian

(Opposite) MY KITCHEN WINDOW 41.3 cm x 53.3 cm (16 1/4" x 21")
(Top) DUTCH STILL-LIFE 38.1 cm x 48 cm (15" x 19")
(Centre) SUMMER MORNING 36 cm x 36 cm (14" x 14")
(Bottom) SUMMER DESSERT 28 cm x 33 cm (11" x 13")

Getting Started

Palette

Chabrian spreads colours around in the slotted compartments of a John Pike palette. She then pulls them into the central mixing area, where she makes up large batches of the colours she expects to use.

Favourites: Alizarin crimson, Naples yellow cobalt turquoise (sometimes mixed with Naples yellow), Payne's grey and Chinese white.

Brushes

Chabrian uses Isabey squirrel brushes in sizes no. 6 and no. 8, Raphäel kolinski sable round brushes in sizes no. 000 up to no. 10 and Winsor & Newton Series 239 synthetic round brushes in sizes no.1 to no.12.

Favourites: Isabey squirrel, sizes 00, 2 and 6, Raphäel kolinski sable round, sizes 2 and 4.

Surface

Chabrian usually paints on Strathmore Bristol 4-ply board, which she purchases in 50.8 cm x 76.2 cm (20" x 30") sheets and cuts to the size of the intended painting. When painting outdoors, she sometimes works on Lanaquarelle hot-pressed paper

Favourite: Strathmore Bristol 4-ply board.

Chabrian warns that hot-pressed paper may seem difficult to work with at first. "The first layer of colours doesn't stain the fibres of paper as it would with cold-pressed or rough paper. For that reason, the second and third washes can reactivate the first ones and cause the colours and edges to change. It took me a lot of practise to become comfortable with the paper."

Because the pigment never completely settles into the fibres of the paper, Chabrian is able to start painting with broad washes of colour and gradually sharpen edges as she would if painting with oil paints. "I save the white shapes by covering them with frisket, block in the large areas of light colour and then break those into smaller and darker forms without worrying about losing my lighter values or clean edges," she says.

Chabrian makes a point of using one colour to dominate the picture, two others to play secondary roles in the composition and splashes of other colours throughout the picture. "For example, I was thinking about the earthy reds that became the focus of attention in the still life shown here in stages of development," she explains. "The ochres cover more of the paper, but it's those reds that grab the viewer's attention, followed by the whites, blues and greens."

Balancing Related Colours

1 ▶

Chabrian makes a detailed pencil drawing of the still life and applies liquid frisket to preserve the white paper in certain areas. She then works pale, warm washes of yellow ochre, Chinese white, reds and blues over the entire sheet of Bristol board. The first washes of harmonious colours seal the paper so it won't be stained by subsequent colours.

ADVICE FROM THE ARTIST

Always have a good amount of pigment in your brush when you touch it to the surface of hot-pressed paper. Too much water in the mixture may cause you to lift off paint when you're trying to lay more on.

2 ▲

Still working the entire paper, Chabrian paints pale, warm washes of yellow ochre mixed with Chinese white and adds small amounts of reds and blues. She then establishes general areas of colour with loose, broad washes of reds, greens, blues and ochres.

squirrel brush

Deborah L. Chabrian

The artist begins to get more specific about colours and values, painting pale blues and greens in the areas of reflected light and shadow. She allows the colours to mix spontaneously on the paper to create colour harmony and the 'beautiful accidents of watercolour'.

Chabrian now makes an effort to paint the exact appearance of each object, using a hairdryer to speed up the drying time and a stiff bristle brush to remove paint where she needs to lighten values and soften highlights

She begins to add interest in the textures and patterns by covering most of the painting with tracing paper and then splattering paint from the edge of a stiff toothbrush on to the uncovered areas. She splatters cobalt blue, Payne's grey, alizarin crimson and raw umber into the shadows for variations of purples and blues.

Chabrian removes the frisket and begins to paint the details and darkest values in the picture. She tries not to finish everything to the same degree because she finds it more interesting if some areas are less well defined than others.

She washes warm colours over the flowerpot in the window, and paints darker tones into the light areas near the board under the grapes. After she adds a few dark touches here and there, she decides the painting is finished and paints her signature.

BALANCING RELATED COLOURS

Colour Mixing Workshop

Different Colour Mixtures

Chabrian painted all four of these watercolours with mixtures of cobalt blue, ultramarine blue, permanent rose, yellow ochre and Chinese white. Notice how the different mixtures change the presentation of the same object.

The magic trick Deborah L. Chabrian can teach you is how to get the maximum effect from a few colour mixtures. To come up with all the reds, blues, yellows, greens, purples, oranges and greys she needs to complete her still-life paintings, she uses just a few well-chosen tube colours. She works with yellow ochre, raw sienna, permanent rose, Chinese white and three blues to perform that magic.

> *The magic trick Deborah L. Chabrian can teach you is how to get the maximum effect from a few colour mixtures.*

Chabrian offers another illustration of the surprising things you can do with a few tube colours. Using a warm and a cool blue (cobalt and ultramarine respectively) one red, one yellow and Chinese white, she paints the same still-life object four times. The subtle shifts in mixtures and the changing placements of the colours have a dramatic impact on the resulting images.

32   COLOUR MIXING FOR STILL LIFES

All of this should give you a sense of freedom in the way colours can be mixed and applied to your paintings. Chabrian shows how to create your own unique paintings with just the slightest shifts in colour, value and placement. Whether you select the same palette or one that suits your own preferences, the impact will be the same.

Subtle Distinctions

Chabrian achieves subtle distinctions by mixing colours with Chinese white and applying them over a tone of yellow ochre. She paints the central panel with yellow ochre, adding mixtures of raw sienna and permanent rose to the top. To the bottom, she adds mixtures of Winsor blue, cobalt blue and ultramarine blue.

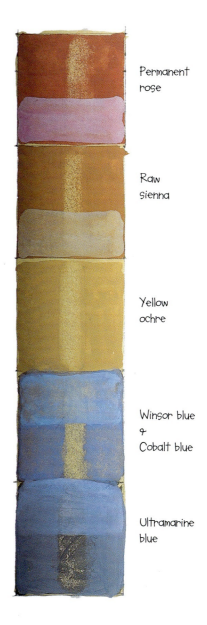

Permanent rose

Raw sienna

Yellow ochre

Winsor blue & Cobalt blue

Ultramarine blue

(Opposite) MAY FLOWERS 26 cm x 33 cm (11" x 13")
(Above) LATE SUMMER FLOWERS 41 cm x 30 cm (16" x 12")

BALANCING RELATED COLOURS

Shaping Objects with Colour

"Painting with watercolour can be compared to laying sheets of coloured cellophane on a light box. Each new colour combines with those underneath and blocks out a little more of the light coming from within the box."

– **Denise Lisiecki**

Although watercolour paints don't perform exactly like layers of cellophane, Denise Lisiecki's analogy helps in understanding how each new colour applied to the watercolour paper affects the developing painting. The choice of colour, manner of application and sequence of layers alter the light penetrating through the paint and reflecting off the white paper.

Lisiecki finds colour charts helpful in selecting the right colours for each new mixture. She makes these herself by painting each colour full strength at one end of a horizontal line, and then gradually diluting it as she extends the line. The charts show her not only what each colour looks like and how transparent it is, but also the variations that exist between brands. One company's cadmium yellow differs slightly from the cadmium yellow manufactured by other companies.

All of this information about transparent and translucent colours helps Lisiecki establish the three-dimensional appearance and surface texture of the still-life objects in her setups. To create these convincing illusions, she establishes the shadows by layering the colours she has chosen over a carefully drawn pattern on the watercolour paper. Lisiecki uses her remarkable command of the watercolour language to communicate to viewers what she finds curious, amusing, elegant, disturbing or joyous about the pieces she depicts. She chooses still-life objects that represent something she wants to share with other people; they may capture the memory of someone who has died, recall artefacts of a foreign culture or celebrate appealing forms that complement one another.

Paintings in this chapter by Denise Lisiecki

(Opposite) VIEW OF THE STUDIO 54 cm x 39.4 cm (21 1/4" X 15 1/2")
(Top) IRIS IN SHADOWS 53. 3 cm x 68.6 cm (21" x 27")
(Centre) WATER CONTAINERS 69.9 cm x 99 cm (27 1/2" X 38 3/4")
(Bottom) CHRYSANTHEMUM IN BLACK BOWL 121.9 cm x 81.3 cm (48" x 32")

Getting Started

Palette

Lisiecki squeezes the colours into plastic or porcelain dishes. By the time she completes a painting, she usually has five or six dishes of paint.

Favourites: Madder carmine and alizarin green. If you find alizarin green too intense, use it over greens that need more vitality, like Hooker's green light.

Brushes

Lisiecki uses a wide brush to apply water in a controlled manner, and adds the paint with a size no. 6 or no. 8 round Kolinsky sable brush. These brushes hold a large amount of colour, release it gradually as the artist applies pressure and then come back to a point.

Favourites: Size no.6 round Kolinski sable brushes.

Surface

Lisiecki has tried a number of papers, but has found Arches the best in accepting a lot of paint before the colours start to become opaque. Arches also releases paint when she needs to lighten certain areas.

Favourite: Arches 140 lb cold-pressed paper, cut from large rolls.

Lisiecki paints standing at a large draughting table. She usually tilts the table back at a 45-degree angle, but she lays it flat when applying a wash to a large area and raises it to a vertical position when striving for a thin layer of colour. To the side of the table, she sets up her still life, illuminated by spotlights that she can move to create different patterns of light and shadow. Lisiecki works from life, not photographs.

Lisiecki arranges and rearranges objects until the selection and composition satisfy her. She is guided both by the message she wants to convey and by the relationship of shapes, colours, patterns, spaces and textures. When she is finally satisfied with the setup, she makes a thumbnail sketch in pencil to evaluate the balance of shapes and values.

Lisiecki then produces a scale drawing of the intended painting so she can make a final determination of the placement and two-dimensional rendering of each object. She transfers the lines of the final drawing to a sheet of watercolour paper taped to her draughting table. She never soaks the entire sheet of paper, but rather paints one shape with clear water before applying paint to that portion of the paper.

Shaping Objects with Colour

 1

Lisiecki staples a sheet of Arches 140 lb cold-pressed paper to a board and carefully draws the outlines of the shapes of her still-life subjects with a 2H graphite pencil. She works freehand (rather than from a traced drawing), referring to the objects themselves and her thumbnail sketch of the overall composition.

 2

Using Schmincke neutral tint, she paints the shadows established by the folds of the fabric. Because of its purple-grey tone, neutral tint works well in establishing both the warm shadows of the white fabric and the red checks. If Lisiecki were to use green, red's complement, she wouldn't be able to carry the shadows from the red checks into the folds of the white checks.

3

After painting the pear shapes with clear water, Lisiecki floats cadmium yellow light into those shapes to establish the base of a warm inner glow. She paints the same yellow on the apple shapes to give the green apples a cool yellow tint, and adds a translucent layer of Schmincke madder carmine to the lighter checks of the fabric.

Denise Lisiecki

4

Lisiecki uses Rowney alizarin green – which she considers the closest tube colour to a pure green – to shade the red pears. She will later paint the pears with Schmincke madder carmine. She tints the green apples with Winsor & Newton mauve because that colour darkens its complement, yellow, in the green used for the apples.

5

The artist layers Schmincke madder carmine once over the pears in the foreground and twice over the pear in the background, allowing the paper to dry completely before painting the second layer. She applies Cotman sap green to the apple on the right. Next Lisiecki paints an opaque layer of Schmincke madder carmine over the darker checks. She then adds Winsor & Newton Davy's grey and Schmincke madder carmine inside the silver bowl.

6

Lisiecki washes another layer of Schmincke madder carmine over the pears and paints an additional layer of Cotman sap green on the apples. She applies Schmincke madder carmine, Winsor & Newton Davy's grey and Cotman sap green to the silver bowl.

COLOUR MIXING FOR STILL LIFES

7

Lisiecki washes the apples in the foreground with Cotman sap green and while the paint is still wet, tips in Winsor & Newton rose carthame to create the reddish orange reflections on the silver bowl.

8

As Lisiecki refines the painting, she paints thin lines between the checks using Schmincke indigo; the darker areas of the green apples with Rowney alizarin green; the dark areas of the pears with Winsor & Newton alizarin crimson; and the darker areas of the bowls with Schmincke lamp black.

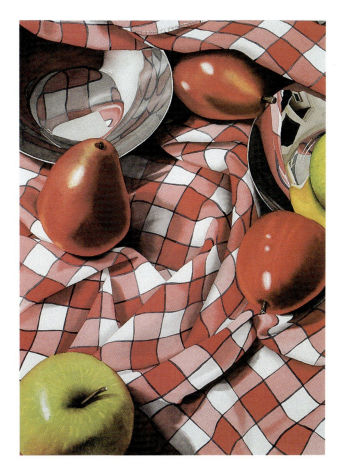

9

Lisiecki feels the colours need to be intensified, so she adds a wash of cadmium yellow light to the pears and alizarin green to their shadows. She also creates the reflections in the silver bowls with Winsor & Newton Davy's grey and a mixture of that grey with black.

SHAPING OBJECTS WITH COLOUR

Colour Mixing Workshop

Three-Dimensional Appearance

Lisiecki uses several tube greys to establish the three-dimensional appearance of objects. For the folds of the chequered fabric, she first paints a neutral tint, a grey that has a purple cast.

Metallic Colour

To create the metallic look of the silver bowl, Lisiecki first paints washes of Davy's grey, a tube colour that leans towards a cool black, and then adds lamp black to finish the painting.

Denise Lisiecki applies watercolour in distinct layers, with each colour wash being allowed to dry thoroughly before the next is applied. That procedure allows the artist to slowly build up the surface of her pictures, gradually increasing the intensity of the colour and the illusions of depth and dimension.

> *Denise Lisiecki applies watercolour in distinct layers, with each colour wash being allowed to dry thoroughly before the next is applied.*

Lisiecki points out a few things that you might not think about when mixing colours. First, she shows the benefit of underpainting colours that will shift the final layers of paint towards a particular colour (in this case, yellow) or towards a warm or cool tone. Next, she demonstrates how painting more than one layer of the same colour will increase the intensity of that colour shape. Finally, she shows how the use of complementary colours will build shadows.

Because this approach depends on careful planning and a

thorough knowledge of colour relationships, it is helpful to make sketches and paint value studies, to keep colour charts and try out colour combinations on test swatches of watercolour paper before adding them to a developing painting.

(Opposite) HOPE, FAITH & INSPIRATION 29.2 cm x 24.8 cm (11½" x 17½")
(Above) MAKING OF A STILL LIFE 124.5 cm x 81.3 cm (49" x 32")

Underpainting

One of the keys to Lisiecki's technique is underpainting a colour that has a subtle impact on the ultimate appearance of an object. A wash of cadmium yellow light and alizarin green on the pear before applying the madder carmine, gives the red of the pear a slightly yellow cast.

Shadows

Lisiecki uses mauve to paint the shadows of the green apples and then applies washes of alizarin green.

Dimensions

To give dimension to the red apple, the artist paints the shadows green and then applies washes of madder carmine

Layers of Colour

To distinguish one red from another, Lisiecki paints only some of the fruit with more than one layer of madder carmine. Notice how two or three layers of the red deepen the value and intensity of the colour.

Schmincke madder carmine

SHAPING OBJECTS WITH COLOUR

CAT *Jean Grastorf,* 50.8 cm x 71 cm (20" x 28")

Colour

Mixing

for

Florals

Flowers are some of the most brightly coloured objects in nature, so artists who paint them have an opportunity to use intense pinks, purples, reds, yellows and oranges – often when painting the same blossom! An artist painting florals can use colours full strength without toning them down, making it easier to experiment with the new, strangely named pigments such as quinacridones, iridescents and metallics

Achieving that brightness and intensity in a unified composition is not a simple matter. Hot reds and royal blues can be tough to pull together without becoming garish, unnatural and silly. Sometimes artists have to build up layers of colour gradually, ensuring that the different tones work together as the painting develops. At other times, they need to intermix colours on the watercolour paper, making sure the pigments blend without becoming a dull grey

The three accomplished artists featured in this section offer different approaches to capturing the liveliness of flowers. All three women are quite deliberate about their techniques; this restraint helps them contend with strong colour choices.

Susan Headley Van Campen is direct and controlled in her use of floral colours. In painting long green stems, flowing leaves and delicate blossoms, she mixes several colours together on her palette, and then makes a limited number of brush strokes on the watercolour paper. These combined pigments realistically capture what the artist sees in front of her.

Mary Weinstein selects from many tube colours when she paints the flowers from her garden. She builds up layers of those colours until she achieves the intensity and brilliance of the real blossoms. Weinstein knows how each colour will perform by itself and in combination with the other colours.

Jean Grastorf developed a novel approach to watercolour – she pours intense, staining colours across a prepared sheet of paper as if she were dyeing a piece of fabric. As a result, the colours remain clean, transparent and brilliant. Not every tube colour will work, however. Grastorf explains her technique below.

MORNING POND *Jean Grastorf*, 102 cm x 76.2cm (40" X 30")

Maximizing Colour Mixtures

"I put together strong mixtures of colour on the palette and make one stroke to describe each stalk, leaf and blossom. It's important to be direct when trying to capture the spirit of the flowers growing in my garden."

– Susan Headley Van Campen

Everything about Susan Headley Van Campen's approach to painting flowers in watercolour is deliberate, uncomplicated and immediate. This observation is especially true of her selection and application of colours. She intermixes a number of pigments on a palette until she gets just the right colour and intensity. She then applies that colour to the paper with a large brush so it accurately describes the subject in front of her.

"I'm interested in the spirit of flowers as they grow, not in their environment or in their botanical detail," Van Campen explains. "I want my paintings to capture their life, not the absolute details of the appearance. Most of the flowers are ones I've grown in my garden because their colours, shapes and textures appeal to me. The fact that I've been involved in their complete life cycle is important to my paintings of them."

Van Campen emphasizes that colour is the most important aspect of the flowers she selects for her garden. She searches for unusual varieties of sunflowers, tulips, irises and poppies to plant in her garden so the colours will be more interesting than those of the flowers available from florists.

*Paintings in this chapter by
Susan Headley Van Campen*

(Opposite) PARROT TULIPS 60 cm x 76.2 cm (22" X 30")
(Top) GLADIOLUS – AUGUST 56 cm x 76.2 cm (22" x 30")
(Centre) VERSCILLAS IN A VASE 56cm x 76.2 cm (22" x 30")
(Bottom) BLACK IRIS 56 cm x 76.2 cm (22" x 30")

Getting Started

Palette

Van Campen mixes colours on her palette, gradually adding pigments. When painting a leaf, she may start with sap green and add cerulean blue if the leaf has a bluish cast. She doesn't use siennas or umbers, but instead mixes Winsor violet and cadmium yellow medium to capture the browns of nature.

Favourite: Winsor violet.

Brushes

Van Campen buys inexpensive Utrecht no. 12 white nylon sable brushes by the dozen and gives them to her children when they lose their shape.

Favourites: Utrecht no. 12 white nylon sable brushes.

Surface

Van Campen prefers Arches 300 lb cold-pressed paper laid flat on the studio floor or an outdoor blanket. She paints on 55.9 cm x 76.2 cm (22" x 30") or 101.6 cm x 152.4 cm (40" x 60") sheets of paper. She doesn't soak the paper or tape it on a rigid surface.

Favourite: Arches 300 lb cold-pressed paper.

Van Campen paints as many watercolours as she can during the summer and autumn when her garden is in bloom. She usually lays a blanket on the ground in the garden, spreads her supplies around her and sits cross-legged on the blanket while she paints. When working from plants in her garden, Van Campen usually paints the stalks all the way to the bottom edge of the paper to suggest growing plants, no cut flowers.

Although she would prefer to paint with the sun shining directly on her paper, Van Campen sits under an umbrella so the glare won't hurt her eyes. She doesn't do any preliminary drawing, preferring just to start painting one flower and move on to the next until she has filled the paper. If the blossoms are likely to change quickly, she paints them before the leaves and stalks. "I only work from life, so I have to adjust to the fact that while leaves may last several days, flowers will change within a period of a few hours as the temperature rises or falls," she explains.

In the winter, Van Campen travels from her home in rural Maine to Boston, where she buys unusual flowers from florists and takes them back to her studio. She then breaks from her normal routine of working on one painting at a time and starts several still-life paintings to get as much done as possible before the cut flowers die.

Maximizing Colour Mixtures

 1

Van Campen begins working in her studio from three pots of forced parrot tulips when only three of the blossoms have opened. She uses a transparent mixture of cadmium yellow medium, sap green, Winsor violet and a little Naples yellow to begin painting the leaves and stems.

Advice from the Artist

Prepare strong mixtures of colour and paint each part of the flower with one stroke of the brush. Don't go back over the painted shapes unless they seem too weak or the edges are too soft. Your colour mixtures will have the greatest impact if you limit yourself to one or two layers of paint.

 2

After painting three petals with ruffled edges, she goes back to darken some of the edges with a mixture of Winsor red and rose dore. She quickly adds this mixture to introduce a feature of red into each petal.

A mixture of Winsor red and rose dore is added to each petal

MAXIMIZING COLOUR MIXTURES 49

Susan Headley Van Campen

3

Van Campen now paints more leaves, stems and buds with a mixture of cadmium yellow, sap green and Winsor violet. She adds a little French ultramarine blue to the mixture to paint the darker areas. She brushes touches of Winsor red on to the opening of the ruffled buds.

 4

Painting more of the leaves and two sets of petals on the first two tulips, Van Campen uses the same colours that are already on her palette. She mixes these colours again to aid a second layer of colour on two tulip buds.

5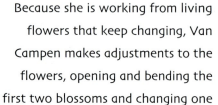

Because she is working from living flowers that keep changing, Van Campen makes adjustments to the flowers, opening and bending the first two blossoms and changing one blossom from a green yellow with red flames to a more intense yellow with a pinkish red fame.

COLOUR MIXING FOR FLORALS

6

The artist uses Naples yellow to add stamens to the flowers. While the paint is still wet, she adds some ivory black mixed with Winsor violet to the tips.

white nylon sable brush

 7

Van Campen paints more leaves with a mixture of cadmium yellow, cerulean blue and sap green. She then covers the darker portions of those leaves with a mix of Winsor violet and French ultramarine blue.

Colour Mixing Workshop

Combination Greens

Van Campen paints the stems and leaves of the plants with combinations of cadmium yellow, sap green, Winsor violet and Naples yellow.

To get a darker green, Van Campen adds ultramarine blue to that same combination of colours, as shown in the bottom square.

Ultramarine blue added

Sometimes the 'correct' colour mixture is the one that performs in a way you personally find to be pleasing. For example, you might select it because the greens flow well when you are painting leaves, or the browns have a warm tone for painting branches, or the colour mixture just looks good in your paintings. To discover the colour mixture that feels right when you are painting, try all sorts of tube colours and recommended combinations.

> *Sometimes the 'correct' colour mixture is the one that performs in a way you personally find to be pleasing.*

After years of painting, Susan Headley Van Campen has developed a sense of which colour combinations are 'correct' for her paintings of flowers from her garden. Instead of using the raw sienna, burnt sienna, raw umber or burnt umber to paint tree trunks or branches, for example, she mixes Winsor violet and cadmium yellow medium to make a warm brown.

COLOUR MIXING FOR FLORALS

Van Campen often mixes four or five different tube colours to arrive at the exact green, red or yellow that she needs for painting branches, blossoms and leaves. Those mixtures are fluid and intense so that the artist can describe the plant form in one smooth motion of the brush.

Browns

Van Campen doesn't use earth colours – siennas and umbers – because she finds that browns made from combinations of Winsor violet and cadmium yellow medium, such as the ones shown here, are closer to what she observes in nature.

Intense Reds

To describe a flower with one stroke of a brush, Van Campen uses an intense red made from a combination of Winsor red and rose dore.

(Opposite) ZINNIAS AND PEARS – OCTOBER 56 cm x 76.2 cm (22" x 30")
(Top) SUNFLOWERS – SEPTEMBER 56 cm x 76.2 cm (22" x 30")
(Bottom) EARLY POPPIES – JUNE 56 cm x 76.2 cm (22" x 30")

MAXIMIZING COLOUR MIXTURES

Getting Colours to Work Together

"Colours have to work together at every stage of a painting's development. No one colour can 'sing' more loudly than the others or be a glaring shape that doesn't fit in with the rest. I achieve that harmony in the way I mix colours and glaze them over the ones already on the watercolour paper."

– Mary Weinstein

Mary Weinstein discovered the exciting potential of colour in a workshop with the legendary watercolourist Robert E. Wood. Wood showed her how to expand the number of tube colours she used by making sure they worked together harmoniously. That discovery still motivates Weinstein's selection of subject matter, palette of colours and painting techniques. "I stopped painting the subdued greys that resulted from overworking a few colours and I started mixing a wide array of related tube colours. Now those colour mixtures help me capture the excitement I felt about the colours in my chosen subject matter," she explains. "As I apply those mixtures to the paper, I make sure they are working in concert with each other."

Weinstein adds, "I begin painting with the colours I see and then glaze mixtures over them. I may start out thinking I'm going to do something soft, and wind up with brilliant pinks and reds; and at other times, I may plan on a strong contrast of darks and lights and wind up with something subtle."

Quite frequently, Weinstein gets to a point in the painting process where she switches from transparent watercolours to acrylic paints so the colours become even more intense. She seals the watercolours with a light mist of Blair acrylic matte medium, and then applies transparent washes of acrylic paint in a manner that resembles watercolour painting. Because acrylics dry permanently, Weinstein doesn't have to worry that a new layer of colour will disturb those underneath it.

Paintings in this chapter by Mary Weinstein

(Opposite) POTPOURRI DES FLEURS 104.1 cm x 74 cm (41" x 29½")
(Top) WOOD DOOR No. 17 104.1 cm x 74 cm (41" x 29½")
(Centre) RASPBERRY SUNDAE 76.2 cm X 56 cm (30" x 22")
(Bottom) LES NYMPHAEAS 104 cm x 74 cm (41" x 29")

Getting started

Palette

Weinstein doesn't have a set palette of colours or a formula for mixing and applying watercolours. The colours shown here represent all of the various blues that might at some point be used by the artist. She starts with a few primary colours and gradually adds pigments. She seldom uses earth colours or tube greens, preferring greens made from combinations of other colours.

Favourites: New gamboge, phthalo blue, phthalo green and Winsor green.

Brushes

Weinstein uses round brushes in sizes No 4, No. 6, No. 8 and No. 12 to paint washes of colour. She switches to Robert Simmons synthetic hair brushes when working with acrylic paints.

Favourites: Round brushes in sizes no. 4, no. 6, no. 8, and no. 12, Robert Simmons synthetic hair brushes

Surface

Weinstein favours Arches 550 lb rough paper. Because the paper is absorbent, the acrylic paint sinks in and doesn't take on the dull matte finish typical of acrylic colours. She doesn't soak the paper or wipe off the sizing, because she prefers to work on a dry, stiff surface.

Favourite: Arches 550 lb rough paper.

Weinstein works from slides of the flowers in her own garden. She keeps the images in binders so she can select the blossoms needed for a particular painting, often using elements from as many as fifteen different photographs.

She projects the slides on to shapes drawn on watercolour paper, with the pencil lines indicating the size and placement of each flower. She then traces the outlines of the major forms. "In recent years, I've been projecting the photographs even more because that saves time and reduces the strain on my eyes," she explains. She makes print enlargements of the most important slides to use for reference.

Weinstein paints light washes of colour to establish the underlying tone of each plant, and follows up with more intense mixtures. She frequently paints several layers of the same colour over a shape to achieve the intensity she wants or alternates two layers of the same colour with one that shifts towards a warmer or cooler temperature.

The paper remains completely flat and unstretched while Weinstein paints. If it buckles during the application of large washes of colour she flattens it after the paint has dried by wetting the back, laying it face down between clean sheets of paper, putting a board on top and applying weights while it dries.

She uses the same palette of colours in acrylics, with the following additions: cobalt violet, Hansa yellow, cadmium scarlet, quinacridone gold, quinacridone crimson and Jenkins green.

COLOUR MIXING FOR FLORALS

Getting Colours to Work Together

1

After reviewing photographs of the flowers in her garden, Weinstein draws circles on the Arches 550 lb rough paper and projects the selected images into the shapes indicated by the pencil lines. She then paints the first tints: yellows and new gamboge in every area that will eventually appear yellow, green or orange; permanent red in other parts of the image; and washes of cobalt blue in the background.

2

Weinstein uses cadmium yellow and cadmium orange for the yellow flowers and scarlet lake, quinacridone red and quinacridone rose on the blossoms. She paints the sunflower leaves with new gamboge, viridian and cerulean. The hollyhocks receive the same mix, with a little extra viridian added. Weinstein doesn't preserve any of the white paper because she wants the first tints to be the lightest values. She covers the daisies with new gamboge, viridian and ultramarine blue.

3

The artist layers the sunflowers on the left side with cadmium orange glazed over with aureolin; she layers the remaining sunflowers with cadmium orange only. She uses cadmium yellow for the pink hollyhock centres, modelling their form with quinacridone red. Weinstein outlines the daisies with cadmium orange and the leaves with a mix of cadmium yellow, Winsor green and ultramarine blue.

Mary Weinstein

4

Weinstein paints the shadows on the yellow flowers with sap green and quinacridone rose; the white ones with cerulean and cadmium orange; the reds with Antwerp blue; and the pinks with cerulean blue. She uses glazes of cadmium yellow and cadmium orange, then applies another glaze of new gamboge. At this point, she sprays the painting with one coat of acrylic matte medium to seal the watercolour so she can apply acrylic paints.

5

Weinstein first paints the red flowers with naphthol crimson. She paints the other reds with quinacridone red; the pinks with permanent rose and, in the shadows, a mix of cadmium orange and viridian. She intensifies the yellow centres with cadmium yellow. Shadows on the leaves are a mix of cadmium yellow, Winsor green and phthalo blue. The artist brushes in the background with a mix of cobalt violet, cerulean blue and ultramarine blue.

6

To finish the painting, Weinstein uses the same palette of colours with the addition of acrylic soft matte medium. She varies the thickness or thinness of the pigment and glazes over the yellows to increase the intensity. The brown centres of the sunflowers are a mix of cadmium scarlet and Winsor green.

7

To finish the leaves, Weinstein adds Jenkins green to the darkest areas. She uses cadmium yellow, cadmium red and Winsor green for the sunflower centres. She then gessoes out the butterfly and repaints it. Weinstein reinforces the background with a deeper mix at the top (ultramarine, phthalo and cerulean blues), blended with Winsor green and phthalo blue. She glazes over some of the leaves and background to make them blend.

GETTING COLOURS TO WORK TOGETHER

Colour Mixing Workshop

Of the twelve artists featured in this book, Mary Weinstein has one of the most extensive palettes of both transparent watercolours and acrylic paints. Each colour helps her create a certain look, either by itself or in combination with the other colours.

Layering is a critical part of Weinstein's technique. One tube colour is painted into a shape, allowed to dry and then another intense and vibrant colour is applied over the top. The decision about which colour to layer at each stage of the painting's development is based on her judgment of the overall harmony of the picture and on the connection between the real flowers and the two-dimensional depiction of them. Ultimately, the colours have to tell the viewers what Weinstein was feeling about those flowers when they were pained.

> Layering is a critical part of Weinstein's technique.

After first establishing colours with transparent watercolours, Weinstein will frequently add layers of acrylic paint. Acrylics are water-based so they work well with watercolours but they dry

Initial Colour Washes

Weinstein first paints some flowers with a wash of cadmium yellow and then, when that paint is dry, covers the centre with a layer of cadmium orange.

Layers of Red

Here you see how intense the red becomes when Weinstein builds up three layers of red – first scarlet lake, then quinacridone red and finally quinacridone rose.

Mixtures for Leaves

Weinstein paints this leaf, and many others, with mixtures of new gamboge, viridian and cerulean blue,

To add variety and dimension to the leaves she paints, Weinstein mixes cadmium yellow, Winsor green and ultramarine blue.

60   COLOUR MIXING FOR FLORALS

permanently and can be built on in thicker, more opaque layers. Weinstein finds that to be advantageous when trying to achieve stronger colours.

She also uses colour combinations that are somewhat unusual – like sap green and quinacridone rose.

(Opposite) LES FLEURS DE MON JARDIN 74.9 cm x 104.1 cm (29½" x 41")
(Top) GEORGIA ON MY MIND 76 cm x 102 cm (30" x 40")
(Bottom) FLEURS DU SOLEIL 74.9 cm x 104.1 cm (29½" x 41")

Shadows

To create the shadows of certain flowers, Weinstein uses a mixture of sap green and quinacridone rose with the yellow flowers, a blend of cerulean blue and cadmium orange with the white blossoms, and Antwerp blue with the red flowers.

Colour Mixtures for Flowers

To achieve the colour mixtures and layers Weinstein uses in her sunflowers, she mixes new gamboge with viridian and ultramarine blue, and applies them to the paper. She then adds cadmium orange, and applies a wash.

Weinstein mixes these colours to create hollyhocks: quinacridone red for the edges of the blossoms; cadmium yellow for the centres; and a mixture of cadmium yellow, Winsor green and ultramarine blue for the stems.

Pouring Luminous Washes

"With traditional layering techniques, the first washes of colour applied with a brush are bright and vibrant, but the successive glazes begin to get dull and muddy. I solve that problem by pouring washes of three transparent, staining colours using specific procedures."

– Jean Grastorf

After trying dozens of tube colours and as many painting techniques, Jean Grastorf changed her approach to mixing and simply began pouring washes of three transparent, staining colours on a carefully prepared surface. She masks large shapes and small details and then pours washes of those colours. After the first washes of colour dry, Grastorf pours a second layer of the three primaries in a manner that resembles batik fabric dyeing. Finally, she does direct painting with a synthetic hair brush to give definition and detail to the image.

The resulting paintings are defined by thin layers of glowing colour in a wide range of values and temperatures. Cool, dark purples and blues put the deck rails into deep shadow, while warm, bright yellows and oranges bring the viewer's attention to the sunlit blossoms and curtains. Grastorf allows the watercolour paints to accomplish what they do better than any other medium – to bring life to a subject with a minimal amount of transparent colour.

But as simple and carefree as this technique may seem when watching Grastorf at work in her studio, it depends on some specific tools and techniques. During her research, Grastorf found that many colours don't perform well during the pouring process, and that a lack of careful planning and preparation could easily lead to unsatisfactory results.

Paintings in this chapter by Jean Grastor

(Opposite) SPRING FLOWER 50.8 cm x 71 cm (20" x 28")
(Top) SEA GRAPES 76.2 cm x 102 cm (30" x 40")
(Centre) BANYAN IV 71 cm x 50.8 cm (28" x 20")
(Bottom) BROMELIAD 50.8 cm x 36 cm (20" x 14")

Getting Started

Palette

Grastorf squeezes paints into round plastic-coated plates that she tosses out after each session. It's important to have fresh colour. If the paint dries and you try to reactivate it, you won't get the kind of clean, transparent colour you need.

Favourites: DaVinci phthalo blue, DaVinci red rose deep and DaVinci Hansa yellow light.

Brushes

When doing the direct painting, the artist uses synthetic hair Golden Fleece round brushes from Cheap Joe's Art Stuff because they hold a good amount of paint, keep a point and have a firm snap that she likes.

Favourites: Round brushes in sizes No. 6, No.8, and No. 12.

Surface

Grastorf uses Waterford 300 lb rough paper because of its bright white surface and ability to hold washes. She soaks the paper for ten minutes in a tub of water, staples it to a sheet of Gatorboard and then tapes around the edges.

Favourite: Waterford 300 lb rough paper.

Grastorf works from photographs and sketches to make a value study of the picture. She then creates a full-scale drawing on tracing paper, making any necessary adjustments before transferring the image to a sheet of watercolour paper that she has soaked, stapled to Gatorboard and allowed to dry thoroughly. At this point, she masks predetermined areas of the paper. The masking agent Grastorf prefers is the Incredible White Mask.

Grastorf dissolves the three staining primary colours in water, preparing stronger mixtures of yellow because the red and blue pigments can overwhelm it. She mixes a large amount of all three paints so she doesn't run out in the middle of a pour.

The artist soaks the prepared paper with clear water, and then pours the three colours across it. She holds the Gatorboard flat so the pigment can soak into the paper and then pours off the excess. As she pours, she directs the cool colours into the shadowed areas of the picture and the warm colours into the sunlit sections.

When the first layer of colour is dry, Grastorf removes frisket from some parts of the painting and applies it to others. She then pours a second layer, adding warm colours over warm colours, cool over cool to maintain harmony and avoid muddy blends. The sections that receive the second wash become deeper and more intense, while those defined by one layer of colour remain bright and transparent.

Pouring Luminous Washes

 1

A value study helps Grastorf evaluate the large shapes within her still-life arrangement and indicates where she needs to apply the Incredible White Mask before pouring colours across the paper. Using this study and her photographic source material, the artist makes a full-size drawing on tracing paper and refines the shapes within the picture.

photo to help render the still life

▼ 2

Grastorf applies the masking agent to the paper to block the back-lit leaves, the purple flowers receiving the sunlight and the areas that are off-beat in colour and require special attention.

ADVICE FROM THE ARTIST

You can add burnt sienna to the palette, but use it only by itself, not mixed with other colours Also, you can use cadmium yellow deep to warm up an area of the painting, but pour it only once.

POURING LUMINOUS WASHES   65

Jean Grastorf

3

The artist lays the Gatorboard flat so she can pour fluid mixtures of DaVinci phthalo blue, DaVinci red rose deep and DaVinci Hansa yellow light. She gives the mixtures time to stain the paper, and then pours them off. She concentrates the warm yellows and reds in the sunlit areas of the deck and the flowers, and the cool blues and purples in the shadows.

Cool blues and purples are concentrated in the shadows.

 **4**

After the paper is dry, Grastorf removes some of the dried masking material to expose parts of the white paper. She paints liquid mask over other areas that received the first wash of staining colour.

5

Grastorf again pours the primary staining colours over the paper. She allows the paper to dry completely before removing all the masking material from the watercolour paper.

COLOUR MIXING FOR FLORALS

▼ 6

The artist begins the direct-painting process with an expanded palette of colours, using round synthetic hair brushes. She makes a point of applying warm colours over the warm tones already on the paper and cool colours over the cool tones.

ADVICE FROM THE ARTIST

"A gouache mixture can add an interesting contrast to the staining colours. Though I rely on the white of the paper for most of the light values, I use gouache to create some flat matte finish whites."

◀ 7

Using the staining colour poured in the initial stages, as well as the new colours added to her palette, Grastorf continues to add detail, At this point, she doesn't concern herself with the way the actual subject looks in photographs or in life because she wants the picture to have its own reality.

POURING LUMINOUS WASHES

Colour Mixing Workshop

Poured Colour Washes

Here's a simple demonstration of Grastorf's pouring technique. She blocks the white shapes with the Incredible White Mask and pours the three staining colours (DaVinci Hansa yellow light, DaVinci red rose deep and DaVinci phthalo blue). When the paint dries, she adds more of the masking agent to preserve the light colours before pouring a second, darker layer of the primaries.

Painted Colour Washes

Grastorf then paints washes of colour over the initial poured colours, using a synthetic hair brush

Although Jean Grastorf's colour mixing procedures depend on very few tube colours and supplies, they are so different from the others demonstrated in this book that you will want to practise them before attempting a full-scale painting. Do not be surprised if you experience a certain amount of scepticism and anxiety the first time you start pouring diluted paint over the paper. It may seem to be an uncontrollable mess, but with practise you will see how Grastorf is able to get the warm colours in the sunlit areas and the cool colours into the shadows while taking advantage of the random patterns created by the flowing paints.

These are the kinds of simple tests you might want to make to become comfortable with the pouring methods. It will take a few

> *Do not be surprised if you experience a certain amount of scepticism and anxiety the first time you start pouring diluted paint over the paper.*

attempts to learn how thin to make the paint, how to tilt the board and how to exercise a certain amount of control over the results. You will also discover how to anticipate what will happen during the first and second pours, and how you can add detail later with a paint brush.

Poured versus Mixed Colours

The six swatches of colour show how Grastorf's palette of primary colours looks when she pours mixtures on to the watercolour paper. Below the swatches are two squares made with the same primaries mixed together on the palette and painted on the paper. Notice how dull and grey the colours become when mixed on the palette and how vibrant they are when poured.

(Opposite) RHODODENDRON 91 cm x 114 cm (36" x 45")
(Top) BIRD OF PARADISE 50.8 cm x 71 cm (20" x 28")
(Bottom) SUN-KISSED 50.8 cm x 71 cm (20" x 28")

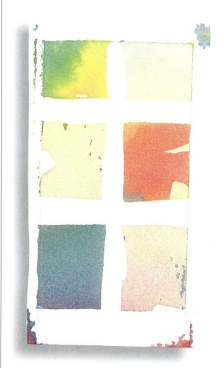

Hansa yellow light & red rose deep, plus phthalo blue

phthalo blue & red rose deep plus Hansa yellow light

POURING LUMINOUS WASHES 69

THE INN, CLUNES *Robert A Wade*, 18 cm x 28 cm (7" x 11")

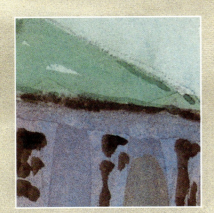

Colour Mixing for Landscapes

Beginning watercolourists often make the mistake of painting trees with Hooker's green dark, skies with cobalt blue and rivers with French ultramarine blue. Eventually, they realize that the colour of objects in nature depends on the weather and atmosphere, the season of the year, the distance between the observer and the object and the quality of light. In the middle of August, the grass should probably be painted with a brownish-green made from a mixture of yellow ochre, raw sienna and French ultramarine blue; the sky might best be rendered in a greyish-blue made from a combination of cobalt blue and raw sienna; and the rivers would seem more believable if painted with a grey-purple made by mixing phthalo blue and alizarin crimson, and painting them on a dampened sheet of paper.

In studying the three artists who contributed to this section, you'll discover ways of understanding and responding to these relative conditions when painting landscapes. Skip Lawrence shows you how to work with strong colours – many of them ones that other artists avoid – to capture your feelings about remembered places. He points out that relative values and intensities are more important than the exact colour of the trees and the sky, and shows you how to determine those values.

Robert A. Wade tones the surface of his paper with light washes of colour before he starts painting the sky or a river. That tone unifies the picture while it warms the highlights. When Wade is ready to paint the various parts of the landscape, he does so with deliberate, calligraphic brush strokes.

Rolland Golden is more methodical in the way he mixes and applies colours to watercolour paper. He prepares each colour uniformly on the palette and applies it evenly to the painting, all in a controlled and carefully considered sequence. He then makes adjustments by glazing over washes of lighter or darker colours.

JANUARY IN VICKSBURG *Rolland Golden*, 76.2 cm x 55.9 cm (30" x 22")

Emphasizing Colour Shapes

"Has anyone ever invited you into their garden to observe the strong pattern of dark and light values? Of course not. They want you to see the colours and not the puny, soft tones or the dark flat shadows. They want you to enjoy the deep reds, the brilliant yellows, the glowing whites and the textural greens."

– Skip Lawrence

For most watercolorists, Skip Lawrence's palette of colours and painting techniques are at odds with everything they have been taught. He does not follow the traditional practise of selecting a specific range of pigments and applying them in a sequence – lightest, brightest colours first, then darkest, muted tones. His approach is simple: first, consider the shapes created by the colours you apply to the watercolour paper; then, study the way one colour affects the appearance of others in the picture. Finally, work with intense applications of colour rather than thin glazes of pigment.

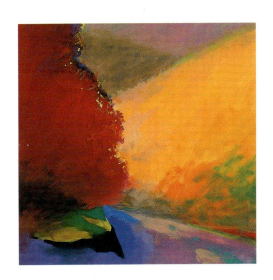

The aim of this unorthodox approach is to create bold, expressive paintings that show what is most exciting in a landscape. To Lawrence, colour is the most important element of watercolour painting. It is the key to presenting his response to selected subjects. "Good paintings are the result of clear ideas and honest passion," he says emphatically. "They are expressions of a particular subject that is seen, felt and understood. Their content (the subject of the artwork) and form (the arrangement of elements) must be considered not as two separate elements of art but rather as one inseparable unit."

Paintings in this chapter by Skip Lawrence

(Opposite) INTRIGUE 56 cm x 76.2 cm (22" x 30")
(Top) COMPOSE COMPOSITION 50.8 cm: x 66 cm (20" x 26")
(Centre) THE EDGE OF ORANGE 74 cm x 74 cm (29" x 29")
(Bottom) GREENVILLE 50.8 cm x 66 cm (20" x 26"

Getting Started

Palette

Lawrence employs up to seventy colours – standard cadmium, earth pigments, cobalts and phthalos, plus an array of sedimentary, transparent and opaque colours.

Favourites: Holbein's compose green and jaune brilliant – toothpaste-thick, opaque colours that are not for purists. He uses them to enhance colour intensity and to adjust colour relationships, not to correct mistakes.

Brushes

Large, oil painting-style brushes – synthetic or bristle – let the artist control how much water mixes with the paint, and help him move pigment around on the damp watercolour paper.

Favourites: Large No. 10 and No. 12 sable brushes, stiff 2 cm (1½") and 5 cm (2") bristle brushes, and 5 cm (2") Skipper brushes for painting backgrounds.

Surface

Rough watercolour paper is best for this technique; paint sinks into the fibres and creates soft edges between forms. Rough paper melts shapes together, whereas hot-pressed paper leaves the edges sharply defined.

Favourites: Arches 140 lb and 300 lb watercolour papers clipped to a board or, for large paintings, taped down to remain flat.

Before he begins painting, Lawrence makes four or five pencil lines on the watercolour paper to indicate the general shapes that define the basic elements of the picture. Then he dampens the surface of the paper with brush strokes of clean water and applies a diluted wash of colour over the entire sheet of paper – usually a warm tone of yellow ochre or cadmium yellow medium. The damp surface is essential to this technique because it allows the colour to be thoroughly absorbed into the paper and creates soft edges between the painted forms.

Lawrence does not preserve parts of the white paper for the lightest value in his picture, avoiding the stark contrast of colour laid next to the sharp edges of a white shape. Once he applies the washes, his focus shifts to breaking the picture up into a few large shapes, using transparent colours like cobalt blue. Then he adds specific elements of the scene – more to balance the relationship of warm and cool colours, bright and grey tones, and intense and subtle pigment dispersals than to add detail.

The landscape shown in the demonstration isn't based on a particular place, but rather on a number of memorable streams where Lawrence has gone fly-fishing – it represents more of a feeling than a particular view.

Emphasizing Colour Shapes

Pencil lines beneath wash

 1

Beneath a middle-value wash of yellow ochre, a few pencil lines identify the large shapes and directional movements within the picture.

 2

While the first colour is still wet, Lawrence applies a glaze of cadmium red diluted to the same value as the yellow ochre. "The secret to the successful layering of colour is applying washes of the same value and controlling the amount of water on the brush," he explains.

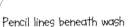

ADVICE FROM THE ARTIST

Try not to get too involved in the small patterns within shapes. Many paintings fail because the artist got lost in painting windows, doors or branches, instead of the overall relationship of the large shapes.

5 cm (2") Skipper brush for painting backgrounds

Skip Lawrence

3 ▶

The combined washes of yellow ochre and cadmium red make an orange that warms the paper and creates a sense of light. While the paper is still wet, Lawrence applies a glaze of ultramarine blue of the same value. This neutralizes portions of the orange and creates an underpainting for the landscape.

Yellow ochre and cadmium red make an orange that creates a sense of light.

◀ **4**

The artist squeezes a generous amount of transparent, non-staining cobalt blue directly on to the wet paper and smears it around with a 5 cm (2") Skipper brush to establish a colour dominance and mood.

5 ▶

Lawrence adds ultramarine blue, turquoise blue, permanent rose and small amounts of compose green to the initial shapes in order to contrast with the existing cobalt blue. He introduces the tree trunks using all the previously named colours.

COLOUR MIXING FOR LANDSCAPES

▼ 6

Lawrence adds reflections of colour to the stream, and makes the still surface of the water warmer and more neutral with mixtures of complementary and opaque pigments – jaune brilliant, blue grey and compose green. This develops contrasts with the pure, cool blue of the dominant shape.

When you need an intense colour to dominate an area or to act as a bright accent, squeeze the paint directly on to the paper and either brush it in with a 5 cm (2") Skipper brush or just leave it sitting on the surface.

▼ 7

Hansa lemon yellow, placed above the blue shape to the far left, introduces contrast with the hue and temperature of the blue and harmonizes with the intensity of the hue. The artist slightly darkens the sky shape with a wash of jaune brilliant. From this point on, Lawrence fine-tunes the colour relationships with overlays of warm or cool tones, and he adjusts the hard, soft and broken edges of the various shapes.

EMPHASIZING COLOUR SHAPES

Colour Mixing Workshop

Lawrence says that colour decisions at each painting stage are based on personal preferences. "From my experience, I have an intuitive sense of which colours to use," he explains. "I do believe that students need to find out how each colour performs alone and with other colours. While my approach to colour may be somewhat unorthodox, I still believe an artist needs to know what differences to expect from a cobalt blue, ultramarine blue and phthalo blue, for example.

"You don't need high contrast between darks and lights to create a successful painting. It can come from an exploration of colour relationships, textural contrast, spatial balance and value shifts." Lawrence also notes that colours get less intense as they sink into the paper and dry. To compensate, it is often necessary to modulate colour relationships in the final stages of the painting. One

> 'You don't need high contrast between darks and lights to create a successful painting'.

Value

Value is a critical aspect of Lawrence's work with colour. By varying the amount of water you add to paint, you can control the relative value of the colour: lots of water yields light values, and little water yields dark values, as shown in this progressive scale of phthalo blue.

Phthalo blue

Colours Mixed to the Same Value

Lawrence stresses the importance of using different colours that have the same relative value. To make values match, you may need to dilute some colours a great deal and others very little. Here, the intense purple hue is diluted quite a bit to match the value of the nearly undiluted brown.

COLOUR MIXING FOR LANDSCAPES

approach is to dull some colours with an overlay of their complement (a green over a red, for example), and brighten others with a wash of transparent yellow or orange. Opaque colours can be layered to either darken or lighten the values.

(Opposite) SUMMER KITCHEN 91 cm x 114 cm (36" x 45")
(Top) CARLY 74 cm x 114 cm (29" x 45")
(Bottom) ROAD TO NEW MARKET 74 cm x 114 cm (29" x 45")

Intense Colour

Another key element of Lawrence's approach to colour is working with intense colours on damp paper. The illustration above was painted with intense, staining colours on wet paper, while the one below was made with highly diluted mixtures of transparent, non-staining colours on a dry sheet of paper.

EMPHASIZING COLOUR SHAPES 81

Starting with Tonal Washes

"Painting an initial wash of colour over large areas of the watercolour paper will mellow the pristine whites so the only ones that remain will accent the objects close to the viewer. I use this method because there is actually very little true white in nature."

– Robert A. Wade

A key aspect of Robert A. Wade's approach to watercolour is washing colour over large portions of the paper and going back with strong linear marks of mixed colours to define the elements of the landscape. He applies those strong colours in confident and deliberate calligraphic strokes. "Never will my brush strokes be timid." he says. "If I don't quite know what to do next, I will do nothing until I am positive I have made the right decision, which I will put into effect with confidence'.

The Australian artist follows a rather traditional approach to watercolour in that he usually paints from light to dark values, from thin to thick mixtures of paint and from broad areas to smaller details. But his technique varies in the initial stages of the process because he doesn't save much of the white paper. "In the initial stages of the painting, I like to cover the sheet with washes of raw sienna, cobalt blue or touches of light red as soon as possible, working in big, soft, light-valued shapes and then going back, into some of them wet-in-wet," he explains. "I will require the paper to dry after this stage is over, then I can go into layering and, finally, defining some shapes with more intense colour mixes, using ultramarine blue or alizarin crimson in combination with other colours to give a thicker, dark mix. I try to achieve a variety of soft and hard edges, with some dry-brush effects for contrast."

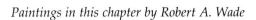

Paintings in this chapter by Robert A. Wade

(Opposite) TUMUT TRACK 38 cm x 51 cm (15" x 20")
(Top) THE CHARLES BRIDGE, PRAGUE 38 cm x 51 cm (15" x 20")
(Centre) THE WALL OF CHINA 38 cm x 51 cm (15" x 20")
(Bottom) SPIRES OF PRAGUE 36 cm x 25 cm (14" x 10")

Getting Started

Palette

Wade uses about three times as much cobalt blue as any other colour because it mixes so well with other pigments to create beautiful greys, greens, mauves and subtle browns that are transparent and non-staining He also mixes raw sienna with other colours to make excellent greys and greens.

Favourites: Cobalt blue and raw sienna.

Brushes

He prefers Robert A. Wade signature white nylon brushes (available only in Australia): 1½" flat and No. 6, No. 8, No. 12 and No. 16 rounds. He also uses Winsor & Newton Series 7 Kolinsky round sables in all sizes from No. 4 to No. 14.

Favourites: Robert A. Wade white nylon brushes.

Surface

Wade usually works with Arches, Lanaquarelle, Fabriano, Bockingford or David Cox paper.

Favourite: Waterford, because he likes the way it accepts washes of colour and releases them if the values need to be lightened.

Wade tapes his paper to a board, rubbing the tape so it won't lift. He never soaks the paper, but frequently wets specific areas with clear water using a flat brush. In his studio, the artist works at a custom-made painting desk illuminated by lights that approximate sunlight; when outdoors, he uses a portable easel. Wade stands while painting because it allows him to step back to evaluate the developing image. Using his quick studies and compositional drawings, Wade sketches in the basic outlines of the shape he intends to paint, and then brushes on heavily diluted mixtures of colours that cover most of the paper. For example, he might use a pale wash of raw sienna in the sky area to establish a warm underpainting for the blue, which he adds while the wash is still wet.

In the initial stages, Wade develops light-valued shapes. He builds up four or five washes of colour in an area, keeping each wet so the transparency of the colours isn't lost. He then allows the paper to dry before defining the shapes with stronger mixtures of colour and calligraphic brush marks.

Having travelled around the world almost thirty times, Wade is accustomed to working under all kinds of conditions. He finds his palette of colours versatile enough to capture the light and atmosphere of landscapes from Morocco to Maine.

Starting with Tonal Values

1

Wade completes this 15.2 cm x 22.9 cm (6" x 9") watercolour study and the pencil drawings of the cattle on location in five or ten minutes. He takes photographs of the same scene and brings the sketches and photographs back to his studio, where he uses them as reference material for the large watercolour.

Pencil sketches done on location

Wade prefers a white nylon brush

2

The artist paints a pale wash of raw sienna across the entire sky area. He also brushes in the soft clouds wet-in-wet with cobalt blue and a touch of light red, which turns the blue into a warm grey. Using mixtures of cobalt blue and permanent magenta, he adds the distant hills to the damp, lower portion of sky colour.

STARTING WITH TONAL WASHES

Robert A. Wade

3

Continuing to work down the sheet of paper, Wade applies a warm mixture of light red and raw sienna over the track. He also paints a bright, warm wash of quinacridone gold on the shapes of the cattle, making sure to preserve some white highlights on the animals.

ADVICE FROM THE ARTIST

Let your feelings about a subject guide your selection of colours. If you sense a warm glow, use the bright yellows on your palette. If you are moved by the dark, cool shadows, then mix in the darker blues and purples.

 4

Wade adds trees with a transparent mixture of raw sienna and cobalt blue, building up texture without focusing on detail. He uses a green made by combining cobalt blue and raw sienna to create a dark pattern under the cattle.

Cobalt blue is mixed with raw sienna to make a dark green shadow.

COLOUR MIXING FOR LANDSCAPES

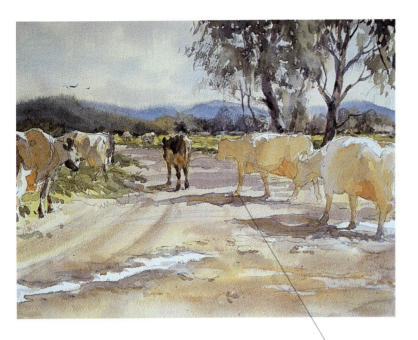

 5

Looking more closely at the cattle, Wade uses stronger mixtures of quinacridone gold, raw sienna and cobalt blue to give weight and mass to the animals and their cast shadows. Washes of permanent magenta and Winsor violet establish the cast shadows of the trees.

Quinacridone gold, raw sienna and cobalt blue add weight to the cattle.

 6

Wade continues to work on the forms of the cattle, darkening the values with mixtures of French ultramarine blue, alizarin crimson and a touch of burnt sienna. He alters the shape of the puddle and adds a small amount of off-white gouache to restore the crisp edge on the dark cow.

STARTING WITH TONAL WASHES

Colour Mixing Workshop

Raw Sienna Wash

Wade often begins a painting by laying a wash of raw sienna over his preliminary drawing to establish a warm tone to the colours applied later.

Raw sienna

Cobalt blue

Cobalt Blue Wash

Occasionally, he applies a wash of his other favourite colour, cobalt blue, either by itself or mixed with raw sienna.

At one time it was quite common for watercolorists to work on sheets of paper that were lightly coloured by the manufacturer. A tint of tan, blue or green served as a ground that gave the first washes of watercolour a warm or cool tone and it necessitated the use of Chinese white or white gouache for the lightest values in a composition. Eventually, those papers were replaced by the pure white papers used today. In recent years a few manufacturers have reintroduced the tinted sheets of paper.

> *Robert A. Wade finds it useful to have a light wash of colour covering his watercolour paper.*

Robert A. Wade finds it useful to have a light wash of colour covering his watercolour paper, but instead of buying sheets manufactured with uniform tones, he paints large areas of his paper with thin mixtures of raw sienna or cobalt blue after his drawing of a subject is complete. These tones help to unify the composition, and because value is relative, Wade can make those tints seem as light as the

COLOUR MIXING FOR LANDSCAPES

white of an untinted sheet of watercolour paper. He does that by keeping the tints thin and making the darks within the picture quite strong. The contrast between those darks and the tints is sufficient to make an effective composition.

(Opposite) HANGIN' OUT, VENICE 38 cm x 51 cm (15"x 20")
(Top) IN SCUDAMORE'S BARN 38 cm x 51 cm (15" x 20")
(Bottom) THE GREEN AWNING, BRUGES 28 cm x 36 cm (11" x 14")

Clouds

Wade applies cobalt blue over a wash of raw sienna to make the clouds. Below are swatches of raw sienna and cobalt blue, along with the mixtures of cobalt blue and light red used in the clouds, and the cobalt blue and permanent mauve combination painted along the hillside.

Trees

In painting the trees, Wade uses combinations of cobalt blue and raw sienna to make several dark greens. Here he paints those green mixtures over a wash of cobalt blue.

STARTING WITH TONAL WASHES

Controlling Colour Washes

"The key to getting a consistent, even wash of colour is to mix plenty of paint, test the intensity of the pigments and the overlapping washes, and stir the mixture thoroughly before each stroke of the brush."

– **Rolland Golden**

Rolland Golden describes himself as a 'control painter', in that he measures, plans, tests and organizes every aspect of his creative process. His watercolours express exactly what he intends because he thoughtfully plans the composition and

the colours. Golden carefully chooses his pigments and applies them to the paper in uniform washes that are usually confined to hard-edged shapes. He also follows certain time-tested procedures for

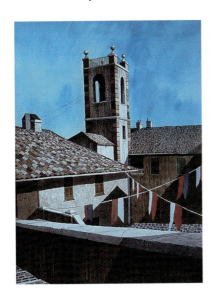

mixing colours. For example, he first dilutes the weaker pigments like cobalt blue and yellow ochre with relatively small amounts of water, and then gradually adds the stronger pigments like Antwerp blue and cadmium red. He tests the combination on a scrap of the same paper used for his picture, either by itself or washed over other colours on his palette. These procedures make it possible for Golden to work with colours that other artists avoid, such as Prussian blue, an intense, staining colour that can easily overpower weaker pigments. Although Golden's slow, methodical technique doesn't lend itself to being taught in workshops or demonstrations, he is generous in sharing information about the way he uses colour in an organized, carefully planned manner. "I personally feel it is more satisfying to create the painting you imagine in your mind rather than one that just happens on the paper. For that reason, I like to have a compositional plan established before I begin to paint and a fairly clear idea of how each new colour I apply will affect the evolving painting'.

Paintings in this chapter by Rolland Golden

(Opposite) SOUTHERN ICE 83.8 cm x 63.5 cm (33" x 25")
(Top) HOLY ROLLS 55.9 cm x 76.2 cm (22" x 30")
(Centre) ST CAGNÉ SUR MER 63.5 cm x 45.7 cm (25" x 18")
(Bottom) WORK IN PROGRESS 90.2 cm x 67.3 cm (35 ½" x 26 ½")

Getting Started

Palette

Golden places a glass palette over a white sheet of paper for mixing colours because it allows him to judge the transparency and intensity of the pigment. He usually mixes one combination of colours at a time unless he intends to apply two separate mixtures and blend them together on the paper.

Favourite: Burnt sienna.

Brushes

The choice of brushes is important to Golden's ability to manage the broad washes of colour and tight edges. Most of his brushes are round and made from sable because sable holds a large amount of colour and releases it gradually.

Favourites: Kolinsky sable brushes in sizes No. 2 to No. 12.

Surface

Golden buys paper in rolls and cuts it to size. He always dampens the paper to remove the sizing. While the paper is still wet, he staples smaller sheets to boards and larger sheets to wooden canvas stretchers. The paper becomes tight and flat as it dries.

Favourite: Arches 240 lb cold-pressed paper.

Golden uses on-site sketches or photographs as source material for the small black-and-white sketches he makes to determine how he will organize the values and shapes within a picture. He may create several of these sketches before finalizing the proportions of the painting, the composition of forms, and the application of colours.

He then draws the image in the sketch on the stretched watercolour paper in a freehand manner, carefully defining every shape. Golden sometimes leaves a white border between the drawing and the edge of the stretched paper so he can use that space to test colours before applying them.

One of the distinguishing characteristics of Golden's paintings is the seamless uniformity of the washes he lays on the paper. Achieving that kind of wash depends on applying even pressure on the brush, connecting one stroke of colour with the next, and maintaining the consistency of the paint. Golden makes sure he mixes up plenty of paint before applying a wash, and he stirs the paint before each brush stroke so the pigment is evenly suspended in the water. He also tilts the painting slightly so gravity will help to pull the colours down the paper as he applies each stroke of paint.

Controlling Colour Washes

1

Golden projects a slide photograph of his subject on to a sheet of paper. He makes a pencil drawing of the landscape to determine the relative value of each section and to make notations about the colours he will use. According to Golden, this method "returns me to the scene".

2

Golden draws the outlines of the landscape forms in pencil, and masks out the white shapes in the cotton fields and some of the tree leaves using Maskoid. He then applies a wash of cobalt blue and Prussian blue for the sky and water and blocks in the background trees with French ultramarine blue, raw umber and Prussian blue. He paints the leaves with yellow ochre, cadmium yellow and Antwerp blue.

 ## 3

After painting some of the darkest green leaves with a mixture of Prussian blue and sepia, Golden removes the Maskoid from the sky. He adds coloured leaves on the right side with a combination of cadmium red, burnt sienna, cadmium red light and cadmium yellow. When he paints cadmium red medium over the blue sky, the resulting colour is a rich crimson.

Rolland Golden

 4

Golden removes the Maskoid from the trees on the left and paints in some leaves. Using a combination of burnt umber, French ultramarine blue, raw umber and sepia, he lays a flat wash of colour over the foreground and middle ground. He then adds a deeper burnt sienna to the tree along the right margin and paints the dark green trees in front of it.

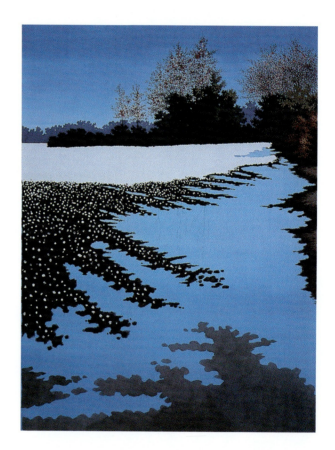

Try to find a specific reason why you want to paint a subject and make sure that everything you do is aimed at showing the viewer what that reason is. Carefully consider the composition of the picture, the choice of colours and the sequential application of washes.

5

Using sepia and burnt umber, the artist paints another layer of colour over the middle ground and edge of the mud to the right. He then places a wash over the bottom area using yellow ochre, raw umber, burnt umber and Antwerp blue. At this point, he removes the remaining Maskoid.

 6

Golden eliminates or reshapes many of the cotton ball shapes to establish variety and depth in the picture. He paints shadows across the fields with a mixture of French ultramarine blue, Payne's grey and Antwerp blue to give the impression of late afternoon light. The artist then decides to remove the yellows from the distant trees by placing a thin wash of red over the existing yellow.

Take advantage of the natural opacity of colours like Naples yellow, cadmium red light, cadmium red medium and cerulean blue. Thick mixtures of those colours can help you add texture or lighten an area.

 7

Golden finishes the painting by adding some variations along the bottom using yellow ochre, raw umber, burnt sienna and Prussian blue. He reduces the contrast in the brown tree on the right and lowers the brightness of the distant red trees by adding more leaves with cadmium red medium and burnt sienna. Golden adds dark limbs to the closest cotton plants and reinforces the darkest black-green.

CONTROLLING COLOUR WASHES

Colour Mixing Workshop

Blended Sky

Golden creates a sky colour by blending Prussian blue and cobalt blue.

Alternative Colours

Artists often find alternatives to their favourite colours when a manufacturer discontinues the colour, the pigment proves not to be lightfast or a similar colour might perform better. For example, Rolland Golden's favourite colour is burnt sienna, shown below on the left, but he can use the new Rowney transparent oxide red, shown on the right, when he wants a staining, non-sedimentary colour that looks similar.

Dramatic changes have been taking place in the manufacturing of watercolour paints, with many colours being completely eliminated or replaced by combinations of different pigments that approximate the appearance of the original colours. Sometimes this is due to the lack of quality raw materials, to the environmental problems caused by the manufacturing process and to consumer pressure to use pigments with higher lightfast ratings.

Two of Rolland Golden's favourite colours (burnt sienna and alizarin crimson) are still readily available as professional grade, high-quality watercolour paints, but they are among the colours that other artists are substituting on their palettes. Those artists are finding inconsistencies in the quality of burnt sienna, and they are concerned about using certain brands of alizarin crimson that haven't received the highest lightfast rating.

Pointillist Technique

Rolland Golden uses a pointillist technique of painting small, independent spots of colour that blend together in the viewers' eyes. Here are three examples of how the same green made by combining Prussian blue and cadmium yellow looks completely different when painted over burnt sienna, a dark blue (French ultramarine blue, raw umber and Prussian blue), and two layers of green (yellow ochre and cadmium yellow, both mixed with Antwerp blue).

COLOUR MIXING FOR LANDSCAPES

So while there is nothing wrong with using the same palettes of colours as Rolland Golden or any of the other artists featured in this book, you may someday find it necessary to consider alternatives when a favourite paint either changes or becomes unavailable.

Winsor & Newton Alizarin crimson (discontinued)

Winsor & Newton Permanent alizarin crimson

Winsor & Newton Quinacridone red

Daniel Smith Perlyene scarlet

Deep Reds

Alizarin crimson is a deep versatile red, but watercolourists are finding alternatives for it because the pigment is not completely lightfast. The first swatch of colour shown above is the discontinued Winsor & Newton alizarin crimson, and the second is the lightfast substitute the company now offers. The next two swatches are other alternatives to alizarin crimson: Winsor & Newton quinacridone red and Daniel Smith perlyene scarlet.

(Top) THREE'S A CROWD 63.5 cm x 88.9 cm (25" x 35")
(Bottom) OUTLIVED & OVERGROWN 64.8 cm x 86.4 cm (25½" x 34")

Mauve (discontinued)

Winsor violet

Ultramarine violet

Mauve

Mauve is another colour that manufacturers are discontinuing. The first swatch shows a true mauve, the others show Winsor violet (dioxazine) and ultramarine violet, suggested alternatives.

CONTROLLING COLOUR WASHES

NENE – HAWAIIAN GOOSE *Jeremy Pearse*, 7½" x 11" (19 cm x 28 cm)

Colour

Mixing

for

Wildlife

Details are of utmost importance to artists painting wildlife subjects, so their approach to colour must allow them to achieve accurate renderings of feathers, fur and leather. Wildlife artists need to select tube colours that match the colours on real animals, and they must apply the colours to the painting in controlled brush strokes. But the need for precision doesn't mean the presentation has to be flat, dull or boring. With a vibrantly coloured background, a lively setting or a focused depiction, the colours of animals can be as captivating as those of flowers or landscapes.

The three artists featured in this section all concern themselves with scientific accuracy in their depiction of animals. They rely heavily on the earth colours – siennas, umbers and ochres – as well as on the various colours of grey. These watercolourists also depend on thoughtful planning, concise rendering and cautious painting of one section at a time. They carefully consider each colour mixture and brush stroke.

Jeremy Pearse mixes lots of water with earth colours like raw sienna, raw umber and yellow ochre so he can wash thin layers of paint on sheets of hot-pressed paper. This approach allows him to build up the colours gradually until they accurately record the appearance of the birds that have captivated him since childhood.

Sharon Weilbaecher uses the techniques she learned as a medical illustrator to mix natural colours for the ducks in her paintings. Her secret is 'floating' the colour on to dampened sections of the watercolour paper. By first moistening the paper with clean water, she is able to glide the paint over her precise drawings.

Colleen Newport Stevens begins her paintings by following some of the same procedures used by Weilbaecher for rendering animals. Stevens then washes brilliant, rich colours into the background to lend a distinctive excitement to her finished paintings. That step helps her create award-winning new paintings or revive ones that she had previously abandoned.

FOX SPARROW Jeremy Pearse, 96 cm x 38 cm (22" x 15")

Detailing with Thin Washes

"I need to be in complete control of the painting process, so I work slowly, building up multiple thin washes of colour and stopping often to assess what I have just completed. That helps me accurately record what I observe in nature."

– Jeremy Pearse

Although the British artist Jeremy Pearse enjoys looking at all the colours in nature, he is only interested in painting the subtle greys, browns, ochres, reds and blues in wildlife. "I'm as captivated as anyone else by the red feathers on a male cardinal or the pink plumage on a flamingo, but I am seldom moved to paint those bright colours," he explains. "I'm more interested in the subtle relationships of muted, harmonious colours. Those seem to convey my feelings about the birds I have observed all my life."

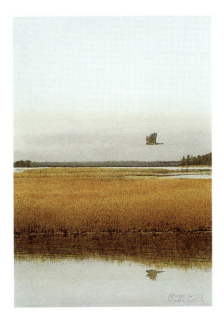

To achieve that balance of colours, Pearse starts painting with thin mixtures of the colours he observes in nature and slowly builds the form of the bird with layers of closely related pigments. He may begin with a mixture of yellow ochre and raw sienna, add a small amount of raw umber to those colours for the next layer, and then mix in a touch of cadmium red for the third wash. He continues this process until he feels the representation of the bird is accurate.

"I don't start out with avalue sketch that tells me how dark or light something needs to be or how intense the pigments should appear," he comments. "I arrive at those decisions as I am painting the animal. That process works well for me, particularly since I am painting on a hot-pressed paper that is unforgiving."

Paintings in this chapter by Jeremy Pearse

(Opposite) GREAT HORNED OWL 18 cm x 27 cm (7" x 10½")
(Top) CRESTED SNAKE EAGLE 18 cm x 27 cm (7" x 10½")
(Centre) HARRIER AT BLACKWATER 27 cm x 18 cm (10½" x 7")
(Bottom) SAURUS CRANE 34 cm x 23 cm (13½" x 9")

Getting Started

Palette

Pearse doesn't include any tube greens on his palette because he prefers to mix his greens from combinations of blues and yellows, modified with small amount of earth colours. He occasionally uses permanent white gouache to lighten values or add fine details.

Favourites: raw sienna, raw umber, cobalt blue and neutral tint.

Brushes

Pearse prefers synthetic hair brushes to those made from animal fur. He uses fairly large sizes, No. 6, No. 8 and No. 10, even when painting small areas. He does have some old natural hair brushes, including a Chinese Sumi-i brush his wife once used, for painting small details.

Favourites: synthetic hair brushes.

Surface

Pearse prefers Arches 140 lb hot-pressed paper stretched on a board. The paper takes some getting used to, so Pearse recommends practising on scrap sheets before beginning a painting.

Favourite: Arches 140 lb hot-pressed paper.

Most of Pearse's subjects are in the fields or zoos near his home, so it is relatively easy for him to study, make sketches and take photographs of the wildlife he might want to paint. He occasionally makes preparatory drawings, but more often than not simply gathers his materials together and begins painting a subject. "I've been studying birds since I was eight or nine years old, and I know when something looks correct or it doesn't," he explains. "I can usually tell from the very beginning of the painting process whether or not a painting will be successful. If it's likely not to be, I tear the piece up and begin again. I'm really ruthless in that regard."

Pearse does almost all of his paintings on Arches 140 lb hot-pressed paper, which he stretches. It took him a while to get used to the hard, smooth surface and the slow rate of absorption, but the paper allows him to paint finer details and achieve the subtle colour relationships he finds so important.

Referring to his sketches and photographs, Pearse does a light but detailed drawing of his subject on the paper, and then begins the painting process. His Winsor & Newton paints are spread out in the compartments of a plastic palette with a mixing area in the middle. He mixes small amounts of colour with generous amounts of water as he begins painting, reducing the amount of water as he nears completion of the work.

Detailing with Thin Washes

Aureolin and cadmium yellow for the eye

 1

Pearse does a light, detailed drawing of the great horned owl and applies two thin mixtures of raw sienna, raw umber and neutral tint to the background. He then adds some aureolin and cadmium yellow medium to the bird's eye; raw sienna and burnt sienna to the lightest area of the plumage; and neutral tint to the darkest parts of the eye.

2

The artist washes Indian red into the area below the eye and aureolin yellow into the eye itself. He uses a mixture of neutral tint, raw umber and burnt sienna to indicate warmer shadows just above the eye and adds a little more burnt umber to the mixture to outline the eye.

Jeremy Pearse

3

Pearse doesn't think the eye is dark enough, so he adds another wash of aureolin to the iris, then burnt umber to the shadow. He paints a mixture of aureolin, raw sienna, and raw umber in the background, and defines the lower edge of the base of the bill with a grey-brown wash.

Pearse adds another wash of aureolin to darken the eye.

4

With neutral tint, Pearse darkens the bill, the ear coverts and the markings on the crown. He adds a mixture of raw sienna, raw umber and burnt sienna to the crown and, after diluting it with more water, to the cheek and ear tufts. The dark quarter-moon shape surrounding the ear coverts receives multiple washes of neutral tint.

5

Pearse washes cerulean blue over the bill and completes the ear tufts with darker washes of raw sienna and raw umber. Neutral tint helps define the feathers and separates the lower edge of the cheek and the darker feathers below. On the back of the head, Pearse paints a thin mixture of the same brown used earlier.

COLOUR MIXING FOR WILDLIFE

6

The artist uses a mixture of raw sienna, raw umber and cadmium red to indicate the palest colouring on the breast and the lower side of the head. He paints the intricate vermiculations on the side of the head with neutral tint and sepia and some of the darker areas with burnt umber.

If you want a dark area of the painting to have depth and richness, paint it first with a wash of burnt umber.

 7

Pearse applies a few more washes of neutral tint to establish the final details, and adds one last wash of raw sienna to the breast.

DETAILING WITH THIN WASHES 107

Colour Mixing Workshop

Muted, Harmonious Colours

To achieve the muted effects that Pearse prefers, he works with closely related earth colours mixed to the same relative value. In fact, Pearse avoids painting animals that would require him adding bright oranges, greens or blues to his palettes.

Raw sienna
Raw umber
Neutral tint

Neutral tint
Burnt sienna

Sepia
Neutral tint

Dramatic changes do not occur from one stage to the next when Jeremy Pearse creates one of his remarkable wildlife paintings. The shifts from one colour mixture to another are achieved with the addition of a small amount of pigment, and the changes from one layer of paint to the next are as subtle as Pearse can make them. He will work with the same three or four colours for days, adding a little more raw sienna for one section of a painting, a bit more cadmium red for the next and a small amount of neutral tint for the third.

Seeing Pearse's subtle colour combinations as separate swatches will give you a better sense of how he works with these pigments to achieve the tight details, soft surfaces and personal interpretation that make his paintings so successful. Remember that Pearse paints on hot-pressed paper, which responds to the colour mixtures quite differently from cold-pressed paper.

(Above) HORNED OWL AT DUSK 20 cm x 28 cm (8" x 11")
(Opposite) GYRFALCON 19 cm x 28 cm (7½" x 11")
(Opposite bottom) SAW WHET OWL 56 cm x 38 cm (22" x 15")

108   COLOUR MIXING FOR WILDLIFE

Warm Mixtures

Pearse varies his colour palette by using warm mixtures of colour to paint both his wildlife subjects and the environments in which they live.

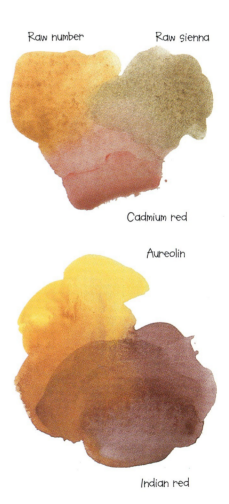

Raw number   Raw sienna

Cadmium red

Aureolin

Indian red

DETAILING WITH WASHES

Floating Colours onto Damp Paper

"I mix colours with small amounts of water on a palette and then float them into shapes on the watercolour paper already dampened with clear water. I also use an airbrush to spray controlled mists of colour."

– Sharon Weilbaecher

Trained as a medical illustrator, Sharon Weilbaecher has an approach to colour mixing that is different from other artists, in that she develops one small section of a picture at a time after first making a detailed pencil drawing. "Medical illustrators are expected to render accurate details and deliver their finished paintings by a deadline, so they learn painting methods that achieve accuracy and develop salvage techniques for making changes." she explains. The proce-

dures she employs help her use colour to establish an accurate depiction of a subject within an expressive painting.

The most critical part of Weilbaecher's technique is floating colours into shapes drawn on the watercolour paper that has already been dampened with clear water. She first mixes those colours with small amounts of water on a disposable wax paper palette, pulling in the paints that she has squeezed around the mixing area. As she floats the mixtures onto the damp paper, the colours sink in and become soft shapes that blend with the shapes around them.

In later stages of the painting process, the artist applies colours on the dried surface of the paper to depict details, or she draws linear features with coloured pencils. She frequently uses an airbrush to achieve the realistic appearance of objects or to unify a background. That tool, powered by a compressor, sprays a controllable mist of colour onto the sections of the paper that have not been blocked by cut stencils or liquid frisket.

Paintings in this chapter by Sharon Weilbaecher

(Opposite) LADIES OF THE LAGOON 66 cm x 92.4 cm (26" X 36")
(Top) SOUTH OF THE RAINBOW 76.2 cm x 55.9 cm (30" x 22")
(Centre) THE LURE OF FISHING 68.6 cm x 66 cm (27" x 26")
(Bottom) MORNING CUP 99.1 cm x 71.1 cm (39" x 28")

Getting Started

Palette

Weilbaecher relies heavily on the transparent, staining colours (Winsor blue, Winsor red and Winsor yellow) because they can be mixed to make bright, clean colours or floated over previously painted colours to change their appearance.

Favourites: Winsor red, Winsor yellow, Winsor blue, cadmium red, cadmium yellow, yellow ochre and brown madder alizarin.

Brushes

Weilbaecher prefers Winsor & Newton Series 7 Kolinsky sable brushes in sizes No. 00, No. 0, No. 1, No. 2 and No. 3 for painting details and No. 4, No. 5, No. 6, and No. 8 for floating colours over larger areas; and Robert Simmons 5 cm (2") synthetic hair brushes for laying in washes.

Favourites: Winsor & Newton Series 7 in sizes No. 0, No. 1, No. 4 and No. 5.

Surface

The artist uses Arches 300 lb cold-pressed paper because it can withstand scrubbing when an area of colour needs to be lightened or removed.

Favourite: Arches 300 lb cold-pressed paper.

Weilbaecher carefully plans her painting before preparing a palette of colours. She explains, "Using photographs of my subject, I make sketches of the elements I am considering, cut the sketches out and move them around on a clean sheet of paper to determine where they should be placed. Once that is determined, I make a value drawing. Then I draw the final image on a sheet of watercolour paper, taking a considerable amount of time to record all the details."

Weilbaecher sprays a workable fixative over the pencil lines so they won't be disturbed by the washes of colour. She soaks the paper, staples it to a board and allows it to dry. Then she dampens one section of the paper and floats mixtures of staining colours.

If an area of a painting needs texture, Weilbaecher splatters colours from the end of a brush while covering the rest of the picture. She also uses an airbrush to spray colour into sections of the paper masked by hand-cut frisket paper or liquid frisket. And if she wants finer details or sharper edges, she adds them with coloured pencils.

Weilbaecher's training in medical illustration helped her develop techniques for altering areas of a painting. For example, she uses a nylon fingernail brush to scrub colours off of one section. After the paper is thoroughly dry, she smoothes the surface with fine sandpaper.

Floating Colours onto Damp Paper

1

After working out her composition on a sheet of Strathmore drawing paper, Weilbaecher enlarges and transfers the image to a sheet of Arches 300 lb cold-pressed paper and carefully draws the details of the ducks and landscape. She then sprays the pencil lines in the ducks with a light mist of workable fixative.

2

After soaking the watercolour paper, stapling it to a board and allowing it to dry, Weilbaecher paints sepia watercolour over the lines of the drawing. Next, she dampens the paper in the area of the ducks' wings and floats a wash of Winsor blue over them.

3

The artist dampens the paper for each duck (leaving the light areas dry) and floats a warm wash of raw sienna mixed with yellow ochre. She floats some cadmium orange on the bills and feet, and then lets the paper dry. Finally, she floats warm sepia on the shadow side and a hint of burnt sienna on the wing.

Sharon Weilbaecher

4

Weilbaecher applies liquid frisket to the leaves, twigs and stones with a small brush, and then floats a combination of Winsor blue, Winsor red and a small amount of Winsor yellow. While the ground area is still damp, she floats burnt sienna and Winsor blue in a small spot of the foreground. Once the paper is dry, she splatters burnt sienna, Winsor blue, raw sienna and burnt umber, using a bristle brush.

5

Weilbaecher now directs her attention to each of the ducks, floating washes of raw sienna, yellow ochre and cadmium orange with a little cadmium red on their bills. She leaves the white of the paper for the highlights and applies thick mixtures of colours to the dry paper to capture the details of the feathers.

White papers highlights

◀ **6**

After applying liquid frisket to the outline of the ducks next to the shoreline, the plants and the cypress trees, she floats separate washes of cadmium yellow pale and Winsor blue. Removing the frisket, she then adds further details to the ducks, using washes of raw sienna, yellow ochre and Winsor blue. She softens some edges by wetting the paper and rubbing it with a cotton swab.

7

The artist wants to strengthen and darken the blue behind the ducks' heads, so she cuts frisket paper to cover the ducks and sprays colours with a Paache double-action airbrush powered by a Badger compressor. She sprays Winsor blue behind the ducks, cadmium yellow in parts of the water and burnt sienna and Winsor red in the tree and leaves.

ADVICE FROM THE ARTIST

Floating colours gives them a softer appearance because they sink into the paper, lose their hard edges and leave the paper smooth and absorbent. When the paper is dry you can use thicker mixtures of colour to paint details over those soft colours.

8

Weilbaecher decides to remove the plants in the background by scrubbing the paper with a nylon fingernail brush. When the paper is dry, she smoothes it with fine sandpaper. She then floats washes of Winsor blue, ultramarine blue, burnt sienna and Winsor red into that area. She adds reeds with gouache paint and lightens the foreground in value by scraping the paper with a single-edged razor.

Colour Mixing Workshop

Without Fixative

Weilbaecher spends a great deal of time drawing the ducks in her painting, so she sprays them with a light mist of workable fixative. This first illustration shows what would have happened if she hadn't applied the fixative - the pencil lines dissolve with the first wash of watercolour.

With Fixative

Weilbaecher sprays this drawing with workable fixative, so the pencil lines remain visible through the sepia colour, painted to further reinforce the lines.

Coloured Pencil

Weilbaecher uses coloured pencils to apply more colours over the drawing and sepia lines.

Sharon Weilbaecher uses a wider range of tools and materials than most artists because her training in medical illustration has acquainted her with a number of special techniques for adding colour to a developing picture. For example, she is the only artist in this book who uses an airbrush to spray a light mist of colour into the background of her wildlife painting. She demonstrates a way of removing part of the painted image by sanding and filing off some of the watercolour paper.

Other special techniques that Weilbaecher uses include spraying a drawing with workable fixative, scratching lines into the surface of the watercolour paper with a craft knife, drawing lines with coloured pencils and painting dry-brush details. All of these are tools with which the artist can create the believable appearance

> *She is the only artist in this book who uses an airbrush to spray a light mist of colour into the background of her wildlife painting.*

COLOUR MIXING FOR WILDLIFE

of her subject – whether it is a duck, a chicken or a human being. Note that Weilbaecher's colour mixtures are applied over a careful drawing made from reference photographs and sketches, an essential guide through the first few stages of the painting process.

Scratching

To keep the linear look to the feathers, the artist employs coloured pencils over the watercolour washes and then scratches lines into the paper with a craft knife.

Mixtures of Primary Colours

This chart shows the variety of mixtures that can be made by combining some of Weilbaecher's favourite colours: Winsor blue, Winsor yellow and Winsor red.

(Opposite) AUNT MOTHA 53.3 cm x 74.9 cm (21" x 29½")
(Top) SUNDAY MARKET 71.1 cm x 76.2 cm (28" x 30")
(Bottom) WAITING IN NEPAL 99.1 cm x 71.1 cm (39" x 28")

FLOATING COLOURS ONTO DAMP PAPER

Mixing Intense, Bright Colours

"I learned to control watercolours by using only a few transparent, non-staining colours and then gradually added intense colours to my palette. I found those strong colours maintained their brilliance if I mixed them on the painting, not on the palette."

– Colleen Newport Stevens

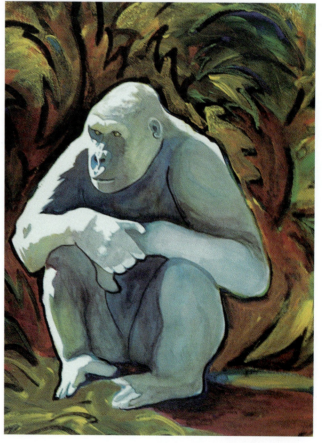

In the competitive arena of wildlife art, Colleen Newport Stevens has distinguished herself by using brilliant reds, purples and golds to capture the vitality of her subject matter. In most of her paintings, she paints a single animal naturalistically with washes of transparent watercolours and then infuses the background with brilliant colours from other water-soluble paints and crayons. She introduces these other media to establish a contrast in the surface texture of the painting while bringing excitement to the play of colours.

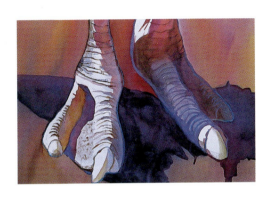

"Once I have established the contrasts of light and shadow with transparent watercolours, I can add more colour with watercolour, acrylics, inks, watercolour crayons and pastels', Stevens explains. 'Those paints allow me to control, change and enhance an image. Furthermore, I create another type of contrast in the textures'.

These colour combinations have proven so effective that Stevens has repainted older pictures to make them more exciting. A few washes of scarlet lake, quinacridone gold or alizarin crimson acrylics or inks in the background of those landscapes and wildlife paintings give them new life.

Paintings in this chapter by Colleen Newport Stevens

(Opposite top) CROWNED GLORY 56 cm x 76.2 cm (22" x 30")
(Opposite bottom) THE THINKER II 76.2 cm X 56 cm (30" x 22")
(Top) DEEP END 56 cm x 76 cm (22" x 30")
(Centre) FEET ONLY A MOTHER COULD LOVE 56 cm x 76 cm (22" x 30")
(Bottom) THE FLAMINGO 76.2 cm X 56 cm (30" x 22")

Getting Started

Palette

Stevens cautions that although painting with intense colours can create exciting pictures, you must control those pigments. When using phthalo colours for example, she often finds it necessary to mix them with other colours, to keep them from 'screaming'. Her acrylic palette includes those colours plus cadmium yellow medium, cadmium red light, azure blue, royal blue and purple brilliant.

Favourite: Scarlet lake.

Brushes

The artist uses 5 cm (2") and 7.5 cm (3") Daniel Smith synthetic hair flat brushes for laying in the initial washes, and synthetic and natural hair rounds in sizes No. 6 and No. 8 for making calligraphic strokes and rendering details.

Favourites: 2"(5 cm) Daniel Smith synthetic hair flat brushes.

Surface

Stevens favours Lanaquarelle 300 lb cold-pressed or rough paper because of its bright white surface, and Arches 300 lb rough or cold-pressed paper because it can take a lot of scraping, lifting and layering of colour. She finds the rough papers absorb colours better.

Favourites: Lanaquarelle and Arches 300 lb rough paper.

Stevens works from her own photographs of animals. She makes freehand drawings of her subjects on watercolour paper attached with large Bulldog clips to sheets of Gatorboard. She then puts the mounted paper on an easel so she can stand while painting.

Stevens squeezes her watercolour paints into two palettes. When working with Pebeo acrylics, she puts those around the edges of a white enamel butcher's tray. When she first began painting with watercolours, Stevens followed the recommendations offered by Jeanne Dobie in her book, *"Making Color Sing"* (Watson–Guptill Publications, Inc.). She learned more about colour and design from Christopher Schink and Milford Zornes.

After three years of mixing aureolin, rose madder genuine, viridian, cobalt and new gamboge to create award-winning paintings, Stevens began using more intense, staining colours like scarlet lake, alizarin crimson and phthalo blue. She also began to mix her colours directly on the painting surface. "When mixed on the palette, the stronger colours can be overpowering and may cause a mixture to become muddy and grey. They are easier to control and maintain their vitality when applied wet-in-wet on the watercolour paper," she explains. "It also helps to keep the painting surface in a vertical position so the colours flow down the paper and interact with each other. Those techniques help keep the colours exciting."

Crowned Glory

 1

After drawing the crowned crane from her own photographs, Stevens begins painting with a palette of transparent watercolours. She mixes cobalt blue and scarlet lake with generous amounts of water to make a dark purple that she washes on to the rough watercolour paper.

2

Washes of new gamboge, aureolin and rose madder genuine fill in the background with bright, transparent colours. These colours become the underlying tone of the intense reds, yellows and purples applied over them.

 3

Stevens uses Rotring inks and Pebeo acrylic paints to create a brilliant background. Because these paints dry permanently, she can build layers of colour until she gets the intensity she wants.

MIXING INTENSE, BRIGHT COLOURS

The Thinker II

Contrast of light and shadow created with transparent non-staining colours

Referring to photographs she took at the zoo, Stevens makes a freehand pencil drawing of the gorilla. She then begins to establish the contrast of light and shadow on the animal using transparent, non-staining colours. She mixes those colours – cobalt blue, rose madder genuine and aureolin – to create a grey colour directly on the rough watercolour paper.

Continuing with a palette of transparent pigments, Stevens paints a background of bright colours to suggest a jungle. She prefers not to refer to the zoo environment because it is so unnatural.

ADVICE FROM THE ARTIST

Learn to work with colour by limiting yourself to a few tubes of paint that can be mixed to make a complete array of colours. The five colours I began with were aureolin, rose madder genuine, viridian, cobalt and new gamboge.

Colleen Newport Stevens

3

Now working with Rotring inks, Stevens darkens the background and the body of the gorilla. She uses intense mixtures of purple for the shadowed areas.

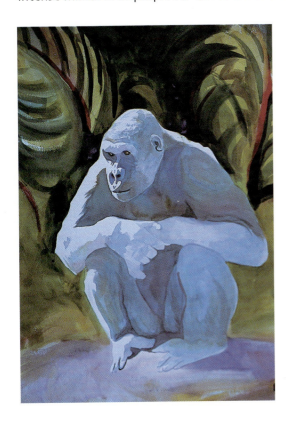

4

Pebeo acrylics allow her to change the foliage in the background completely and introduce some yellows, bright greens and reds into the jungle. She draws dark lines around the animal with Caran d'Ache pencils to help separate it from the background.

MIXING INTENSE, BRIGHT COLOURS

Colour Mixing Workshop

Watercolour Dyes & Liquid Acrylics

One of the techniques Stevens uses to get intense colour in her background is to apply watercolour dyes and liquid acrylics over washes of transparent watercolour. The colours, which are quite intense and brilliant, can be applied with the droppers attached to the caps of the bottled paint or with paint brushes. Here is a sample of two of the brightest watercolour dye colours.

Colleen Newport Stevens uses various colour combinations, managing powerful pigments like scarlet lake and phthalo blue as well as subtle colours like aureolin, viridian and rose madder genuine. The key to her success is using one palette of colours for an animal placed at the centre of her watercolour paper, and another selection of colours for the background.

That intense, atmospheric background is a feature that helps distinguish Stevens's wildlife paintings from those created by other artists. These bright colours are not easy to mix because they tend to dominate any pigment they are combined with. After a little experimentation, you could use these colours to liven up your paintings – even unsuccessful ones you have already tossed aside.

Sunshine yellow and permanent crimson – brilliant concentrated colours

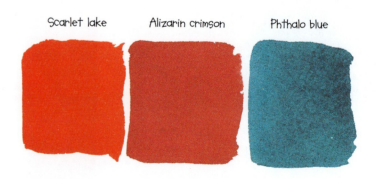

Scarlet lake   Alizarin crimson   Phthalo blue

Outside: aureolin, new gamboge and rose madder genuine

Centre: cobalt and scarlet lake

COLOUR MIXING FOR WILDLIFE

(Top) EMU 71 cm x 56 cm (28" x 22")
(Bottom) THE GATHERING 56 cm x 76.2 cm (22" x 30")

Using Liquid Acrylics

Liquid acrylics can also be dropped into a background to make it more vibrant. They will dry permanently, so subsequent washes of colour will not disturb hem. Here an opaque yellow was painted and allowed to dry before a deep brilliant red acrylic paint was applied over the top.

Yellow gold
opaque acrylics –
deep brilliant red
acrylic paint

MIXING INTENSE, BRIGHT COLOURS   125

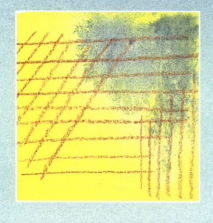

Colour in the Studio

Imagine your sixth-form English teacher saying, "Here are the rules of grammar. Now feel free to break them," or your university science professor encouraging you to circumvent the scientific method. If you were pursuing the study of English or Biology, the results would be disastrous. With watercolour painting, however, breaking the well-established rules and techniques for mixing and applying colours produces exciting and refreshing results – new colours and new techniques to help you find your own unique voice as a creative watercolourist.

This section reconsiders some of the tried-and-true watercolour techniques and characteristics to come up with the best colour combinations for a painting in development. Artists need to know the recommended ways of mixing colours and applying them to watercolour paper. Rules about intensity and value, washes, colour-lifting, brush techniques, colour blooms and combining mediums don't have to be absolute, however. Learn how to break the rules to stimulate your search for creative and effective colour mixtures and to keep your painting fresh and original.

Controlling Intensity and Relative Value

Sometimes the right colour mixture won't produce a successful watercolour painting because the colours don't work well together on the paper. A glowingly transparent green made from aureolin yellow and cobalt blue may look great on the palette but appear weak if placed next to a strong brown made from burnt umber and ultramarine blue. The difference between the intensities and relative value of those two colour combinations is too large.

Artists such as Deborah L. Chabrian and Jeremy Pearse work with subtle differences between the intensity and relative value of their colour mixtures. Others, such as Jean Grastorf and Rolland Golden, strive for sharp contrasts between light and dark shapes. Some teachers tell their students that the 'rules' of watercolour require them to work with thin mixtures of colour, while other instructors dictate the use of intense colours. Ultimately, the best rule to follow is to balance your colour mixtures to suit your subject matter and personal style.

Making value sketches before you begin painting is one effective way to determine the composition of values in your painting, and making colour swatches of your mixtures before you apply them to the paper will give you confidence in the intensities of those combinations.

Thin layers of colour mixtures work together when all of them have the same relative intensity and the values are balanced.

Intense colours are just as effective depicting a subject. Stronger mixtures are used to create the same kind of landscape, but in this case the relative values are much closer.

Even when the colour mixtures are changed radically, their relative intensity and value still affect the outcome of the painting.

Flat and Graded Washes

When colours are mixed thoroughly with lots of water, they can be applied to watercolour paper in uniform, flat washes or in graded bands of blended tones. These carefully painted washes are great for creating the appearance of cast shadows, rounded still-life objects or broad skies.

The 'rules' concerning flat and graded washes call for a generous amount of colour prepared in advance, with the watercolour paper slightly elevated along its top edge, and the colons applied with horizontal strokes of a well-charged brush.

For a more textured wash or more colour variation, you can break the rules by mixing the colours directly on the surface of the paper or applying the prepared colour mixtures in random strokes of a brush.

A small amount of cadmium red is mixed with a generous amount of water and carefully brushed onto a sheet of watercolour paper in uniform horizontal strokes. A bead of coloured water is pulled across the tilted paper so the strokes will blend together to form a uniform tone.

Cadmium red

After three strokes of the same mixture of cadmium red are pulled across the paper, the brush is loaded with Winsor yellow to paint more horizontal bands. The result is a graduated blend of the two colours.

Winsor yellow

A more intense mixture of cadmium red is painted as a flat wash, then Winsor yellow is blended into the red. Finally, the brush is cleaned and pure water is painted across the bottom of the paper causing the yellow to gradually fade.

Cadmium red
Winsor yellow

Lifting Colour

STEP 1: After painting a leaf shape with a mixture of phthalo blue and Winsor yellow, blot the wet surface with a facial tissue to create a random texture. Note that the Winsor yellow comes through in the blotted areas.

STEP 2: Paint the veins of the leaf over the texture surface using the same colour mixture, phthalo blue and Winsor yellow.

STEP 3: To create lines in the leaf shape, blot a wet mixture of cobalt blue and permanent yellow with the folded edges of a facial tissue.

STEP 4: To emphasize the lines previously lifted off the watercolour paper, go back over the leaf with brush strokes of the same colour mixture.

Blotting the edges of a painted shape produces a soft, irregular look quite different front the one created with a brush.

To imitate the appearance of marble, velvet or stone, lift colour from a freshly painted area.

Touching the surface of freshly painted colour with a paper towel, soft cloth or facial tissue softens edges, lightens values and creates interesting textures. The great American watercolourist, Charles Demuth, almost always blotted the wet surfaces of his paintings to emphasize the flat, textured appearance of his still-life subjects.

If you blot a shape painted with a combination of staining and non-staining colours, it's likely you will remove more of the non-staining colour, thus allowing the staining colour to show more clearly. To lift colour with more control, use a clean, damp paintbrush. That technique creates the impression of a rounded form or produces a soft transition between shapes touching each other.

There are a number of unorthodox techniques for lifting colour. One is to sprinkle table salt into a wet area so the grains of salt will absorb the paint and create a speckled texture. Another is to lay clingfilm over an area of wet paint to create a texture without lifting too much paint.

Wet-in-Wet and Dry-Brush

When one fluid mixture of colour is applied to another already on the watercolour paper, the technique is referred to as wet-in-wet painting. As the colours blend together and dry, the edges of the painted shape become soft. That's especially useful when you want a subtle transition between colours to create the appearance of a leaf, a piece of fabric or the fur of an animal.

Dry-brush painting techniques are perfect for adding final details, sharpening the edges of shapes or creating a randomly patterned texture in a rendering of tall grasses. As the name implies, dry-brush applications depend on the colours being mixed with a minimal amount of water so they are intense and opaque. To create thin lines, apply the colour mixtures with a thin, round brush. For a rough pattern, use a wide brush to make dry-brush marks that will skip across textured watercolour paper.

The 'rules' of watercolour say you can't correct mistakes, but dry-brush techniques allow you to paint over areas that aren't quite successful. Because the colour mixtures are opaque, they can lighten dark values, sharpen soft edges and conceal objects that don't work in the composition.

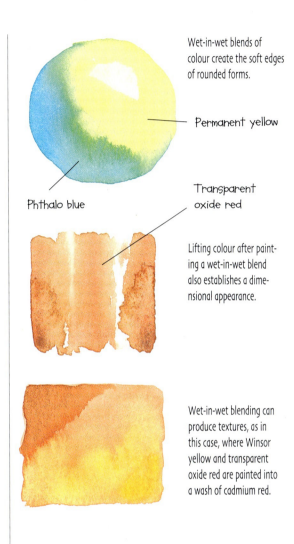

Wet-in-wet blends of colour create the soft edges of rounded forms.

Permanent yellow

Phthalo blue

Transparent oxide red

Lifting colour after painting a wet-in-wet blend also establishes a dimensional appearance.

Wet-in-wet blending can produce textures, as in this case, where Winsor yellow and transparent oxide red are painted into a wash of cadmium red.

A wide brush is used to create a dry-brush texture across the sky, and a thin brush loaded with thick paint makes the tree shapes along the bottom.

Colour Blooms

To create colour blooms, drops of clear water are released into the upper left-hand and lower right-hand corners of a square of wet green paint.

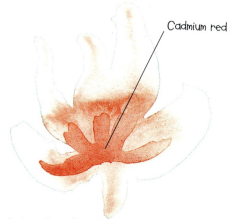

Cadmium red is dropped into a flower shape painted with clear water to make a colour bloom that resembles a spidery blossom.

Blue and green colour mixtures are allowed to flow together across a dampened rectangular shape, forming an intriguing pattern of fluid shapes.

The very idea of working a colour bloom into a painting is at odds with watercolour conventions, yet it is a way of celebrating the flowing, transparent random character of the medium. Colour blooms, or backwashes, are generally considered mistakes because they are an uncontrollable breakup of the colour mixtures. But there may be times when you want to use those 'mistakes' to emphasize the natural flow of the watercolours.

One way to create colour blooms is to drop clear water into freshly painted areas, causing the wet pigment to pull back and collect along the edges of the randomly patterned shape. Another method is to drop colour into areas previously painted with clear water so that the colour will flow into the dampened areas of the paper. A third technique is to drop one colour mixture into a freshly painted second colour.

While the patterns created with these techniques can be random, you can exercise a certain amount of control over the colour blooms by varying the amount of paint, waiting until the first layer of colour is nearly dry, or tilting the paper in one direction or another.

Combining Mediums

Purists will tell you the 'rules' of watercolour dictate creating paintings entirely with transparent watercolour, never adding opaque watercolour, acrylic, coloured pencil or other 'foreign' materials. But in recent years there bas been an explosion of interest in the special colour mixtures that can be achieved with the use of those other supplies.

Opaque watercolour (or gouache) is a water-soluble paint that has more opacity than regular transparent watercolour. It can be used to lighten values, add white accents or correct mistakes. Acrylics, also water-soluble, can be applied to watercolour paper in opaque, translucent or transparent washes that dry permanently. Use acrylics to create varieties of textures, densities and finishes in paintings, or even as adhesives when applying collage materials.

To add finishing details to a watercolour or to create a resist, use wax-based coloured pencils. Create interesting visual effects by drawing lines with coloured pencils and then applying washes of watercolour – the watercolour won't cover the waxy lines.

Lines are drawn with a wax-based coloured pencil and then covered with a wash of Winsor yellow and French ultramarine blue. The wax resists the watercolour paint, allowing the lines to show through.

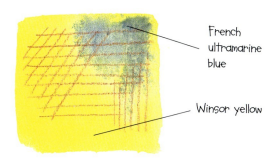

Cadmium red acrylic paint is applied over a square of French ultramarine blue watercolour. The transparent acrylic dries permanently and will not be reactivated by additional strokes of watercolour paint.

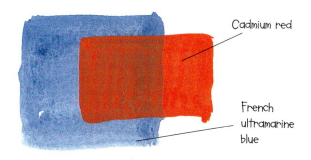

Yellow gouache paint is applied over French ultramarine blue watercolour. Because the gouache is opaque, it covers most of the blue. Both colours would be reactivated by additional strokes of either gouache or watercolour.

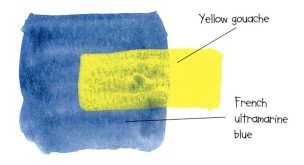

The Best Greens

Cobalt blue + aureolin: a transparent green perfect for glazing.

Cobalt blue + Winsor yellow: a cool green for distant trees.

Phthalo blue + permanent yellow: an intense, cool green for bright plumage or sunlit grasses.

Antwerp blue + Winsor yellow: a subdued cool green for pears and apples.

French ultramarine blue + Winsor yellow: a warm, light green perfect for foreground foliage

The colour green, above all other hues, provokes the most discord among watercolourists. Some artists insist that the only compatible greens are those made from combinations of blues and yellows. Through her pouring technique, Jean Grastorf combines DaVinci phthalo blue and DaVinci Hansa yellow light to make the green colour in her paintings. Tube greens, they argue, are garish and inconsistent with other colours on their palette. But just as many watercolourists find those tube greens – permanent green light, sap green, alizarin green and phthalo green for example – to be far easier to work with than the mixed greens.

The truth is that the best greens are those you find most comfortable to work with. If, like Deborah L. Chabrian, you prefer a simple palette of colours that can be intermixed to give you every colour you need, then you won't need tube greens. But if, like Mary Weinstein, you prefer an extensive palette of all the pigments you might possibly use, then stock up on all the tube greens available.

Keep in mind that some greens are cool and work best when used to suggest distant trees, shadowed plants or hidden leaves; other warm greens are better suited to creating the appearance of sunlit leaves, foreground plants, or highlighted fruit.

French ultramarine blue + quinacridone gold: A warm, olive green for fields of grass.

Hooker's green light: A transparent, non-staining tube green for soft landscape forms.

Alizarin green: A crisp, bright tube green for glazing over still-life objects.

Winsor green: A permanent, staining tube green perfect for inclusion in a limited palette

Contributors

DARYL BRYANT studied with Millard Sheets in Claremont and at the University of Southern California before travelling to Italy to work, paint and study. She earned a degree in graphic design,  and worked as an art director, muralist, sculptor, printmaker and illustrator before devoting herself to watercolour painting. An early teacher, Verna Wells, inspired her initial enthusiasm and love of watercolour. She credits her further growth as an artist to her mentor and instructor, master painter Joseph Mendez. She has participated in workshops taught by Mendez, Judi Betts, Marilyn Simandle, Milford Zornes and Gerald F. Brommer. Her paintings have appeared in juried exhibitions and commercial galleries in California.

Daryl Bryant
1136 Fremont Avenue, Suite 101
South Pasadena, CA 91030
USA

DEBORAH L. CHABRIAN studied at the School of the Art Institute of Chicago before graduating from Parsons School of Design. She later took courses at the School of Visual Arts in  New-York and studied privately with Burton Silverman. Her paintings have won awards and have been included in juried shows organized by the National Academy, National Watercolor Society, American Watercolor Society, Catherine Lorillard Wolfe Art Club and the Society of Illustrators. She is an artist member of the National Watercolor Society, Catherine Lorillard Wolfe Art Club and Kent Art Association.

Deborah L. Chabrian
28 Spooner Hill Road
South Kent, CT 06785
USA

WATERCOLOUR PAINTING

ROLLAND GOLDEN graduated from the John McCrady Art School in New Orleans and became a full-time professional artist in the mid-twentieth century. He is a member of the Watercolor USA Honor Society, National Arts Club, National Watercolor Society, Allied Artists of America, National Society of Painters in Casein and Acrylics, Rocky Mountain National Watermedia, Audubon Artists, and Louisiana Watercolor Society. His paintings have been featured in a number of books and magazines, including *The World of Rolland Golden*, *American Artist* magazine, *Watercolor* magazine, *International Fine Art Collector* magazine, *Southwest Art* magazine, *Louisiana Life* magazine, and *New Orleans* magazine. His works have also been included in dozens of solo and group exhibitions organized by the Mississippi Museum, Butler Institute of American Art, Deland Museum, National Arts Club and other notable institutions.

Rolland Golden
78207 Woods Hole Lane
Folson, LA 70437
USA

JEAN GRASTORF is a signature member of the American Watercolor Society, National Watercolor Society, and Florida, Montana, Midwest, Southern, and Georgia watercolor societies. She has been featured in *The Artistic Touch* by Chris Unwin, *Painting in Harmony with Nature* by Maxine Masterfield, *Artistic Touch 2* by Chris Unwin, and *Splash III*, *Splash IV* and *Splash V* by Rachel Wolf. Her work has been shown at the National Academy of Design. She has won awards in the Rocky Mountain National Watermedia Exhibition and the Adirondacks National Exhibition of American Watercolors. Grastorf often sits on art show juries and teaches workshops demonstrating her technique of pouring luminous washes. Her watercolours are included on the Artscape Internet site at http:\\www.artscape.com.

Jean Grastorf
4th Avenue North
St. Petersburg, FL 33710
USA

CONTRIBUTORS

WILLIAM B. (Skip) LAWRENCE was born and educated in Baltimore, Maryland. He received a bachelor's degree in fine arts  at the Maryland Institute College of Art and a master's degree of arts at Towson State University. He is a signature member of the American Watercolor Society, the Southern Watercolor Society, and the Baltimore Watercolor Society. He authored the book *Painting Light & Shadow in Watercolor* (North Light Publications, Inc.) and is the co-author of *Watermedia Focus*, a quarterly instructional publication sold through Cheap Joe's Art Stuff (800-227-2788).

Skip Lawrence
5000 Old Barthololows Road
Mount Airy, MO 21771
USA

DENISE LISIECKI received a bachelor's degree in fine arts from Miami University in 1973 and a master's degree of arts from the State University of New York at Oswego in 1975. Her paintings and prints have been widely exhibited and collected. Lisiecki's artwork can be found in the collections of the Hickory Museum of Art in Hickory, North Carolina; Kalamazoo Institute of Arts in Michigan; Jesse  Besser Museum in Alpena, Michigan; and Dunnegan Museum of Art in Bolivar, Missouri. She is represented by the Jerald Melberg Gallery in Charlotte, North Carolina; Robert Kidd Gallery in Detroit, Michigan; and Bonfoey Gallery in Cleveland, Ohio. Lisiecki is the chairman of the two-dimensional art department and director of education at the Kalamazoo Institute of Arts.

Denise Lisiecki
3210 Fast G Avenue
Kalamazoo, MI 49004
USA

JEREMY PEARSE was born in Devon, England, and lived in South Africa and Hong  Kong before moving to Gaithersburg, Maryland, in 1993. His paintings have been included in major art exhibitions, including the Mid Atlantic Wildfowl and Wildlife Festival in Virginia Beach, Patuxent Wildlife Show in Maryland, Hudson River Wildlife Festival in New York and Birds in Art exhibitions at the Leigh Yawkey Woodson Art Museum in Wausau, Wisconsin. He is an elected member of the Society of Animal Artists. Pearse is represented by the McBride Gallery in Annapolis, Maryland; Trotman's in Winston-Salem, North Carolina; Massachusetts House Galleries in Maine; and Broadway Gallery in Falls Church, Virginia.

Jeremy Pearse
P.O. Box 2324
Gaithersburg, MD 20886-2324
USA

COLLEEN NEWPORT STEVENS received a bachelor's degree in fine arts from Eastern Washington University in Cheney, Washington. Her paintings have received awards in exhibitions organized by the Midwest Watercolor Society and the Louisiana Watercolor Society. They have been included in Watercolor USA (1994, 1995), organized by the Springfield Art Museum in Missouri, and Birds in Art (1995, 1996, 1997), organized by  the Leigh Yawkey Woodson Art Museum in Wausau, Wisconsin. Her watercolours have been published in issues of *Watercolour Magic* and *American Artist* magazines. Stevens is represented by Madison Avenue Art Gallery in Germantown, Tennessee and Anacortes Gallery in Washington.

Colleen Newport Stevens
8386 Meadow Run Cove
Germantown, TN 38138
USA

CONTRIBUTORS

SUSAN HEADLEY VAN CAMPEN studied at Moore College of Art and the Pennsylvania Academy of the Fine Arts, both in Philadelphia.  Her paintings are included in major private, corporate and museum collections, including those of the Readers Digest Association, the Woodmere Art Museum, the Delaware Art Museum, the Federal Reserve Bank and George Lucas. Her works have also been reproduced in magazines and newspapers, such as *American Artist*, *Down East* and the *Maine Sunday Telegram*. They have also been included in the books *Painting Flowers* (Watson-Guptill Publications, Inc.) and *A Woman's Journal* (Running Press). Van Campen is represented by the Clark Gallery in Lincoln, Massachusetts; Gross McCleaf Gallery in Philadelphia; Priscilla Saunders Gallery in York Harbor, Maine; and Pandion Gallery in Fishers Island, New York.

Susan Headley Van Campen
39 Knox Street
Thomaston, ME 04861
USA

ROBERT A. WADE was born in Melbourne, Australia, where he still resides. He has gained international acclaim as an artist, his watercolours winning over a hundred awards. His work bas been included in shows organized by the Royal Watercolour Society and the Royal Institute of Painters in England; the Knickerbocker Artists, American Watercolor Society, and Salmagundi Club in the United States; and the Australian Watercolour Institute in Australia.

 He was elected Artist of the Year by the Victorian Artists' Society in 1985 and 1986, and received the Advance Australia medal in 1986. He has written two books for North Light Publications: *Painting More Than the Eye Can See* and *Painting Your Vision in Watercolor*. Wade teaches painting in study workshops around theworld.

Robert A. Wade
Dunoon, 524 Burke Road
Camberwell, Victoria 3124
AUSTRALIA

SHARON WEILBAECHER, formerly of Fort Smith, Arkansas, now lives in New Orleans, Louisiana. She received her bachelor's degree in fine arts from the University of Colorado and her master's degree of arts in medical illustration front the Johns Hopkins University in Baltimore.

She has published over 800 medical illustrations. Her paintings can be found in many private and corporate collections.

Sharon Weilbaecher
31 Plover Street
New Orleans, LA 70124
USA

MARY WEINSTEIN is a retired real estate broker. She studied painting with Robert E. Wood,

Scott More, and Linda Stevens and attended the Laguna Beach School of Arts. She is a signature member of the National Watercolor Society and Watercolor West, and has served as a vice-president of both organizations. Her paintings can be found in many private and public collections, including the San Bernardino County Museum and Redlands Community Hospital.

Mary Weinstein
35917 Deerbrook Road
Yucaipa, CA 92399
USA

Index

A
acrylic paint 55,60,119,120,123, 124-125,133
airbrush 110, 111, 112,115,116
alternative colours 96-97

B
blending colours 25,27,96
bright colours 101, 118-125
browns 48, 52,53,84,103
brushes 20, 28, 36,47,48, 56, 64, 76,84,92,104, 112,120,131
Bryant, Daryl 17,18-25

C
Caran d'Ache pencils 123
Chabrian, Deborah L. 17,26-33,128, 134
clouds 89
cobalt blue wash 88
cold-pressed paper 21,27,28,36,37,48, 92,108,113
colour blooms 132
colour charts 35,41
colour distinctions 26,27
colour intensity 20,39,40,41,47,52,56, 73,80-81,83,92,118-125,128
colour mixing 19,24-25,30,32-33,40-41, 52-53,60-61,68-69,80-81,88-89,91,96, 97,108,109,116,117,120,124,-125, 128-129,131,134
colour mixtures 32,46-53, 108,117
colour shapes 74-81
colour washes 60,88-89,90-97
coloured pencil 116,117,133
combining colour 54-61
combining mediums 133
contrast 55,76,78,80,83,119 , 122, 128
controlling colour 17,24,69,118,120, 128

D
damp surfaces 20,24,25,56,73,76,81,84, 92, 101,110-117,132
Demuth, Charles 130
dimension 41
dry brush painting 83,131
dry surfaces 24,38

E
earth colours 20,23,53,56,76, 101,104

F
fixative 113,116
flat washes 129
floating colours 37,101,110-117
finals 42-69
fresh paint 64
frisket 28,31,64,111,112,114, 115

G
Golden, Rolland 73,90-97,128
gouache 67,87,88,104,115,133
graded washes 129
Grastorf, Jean 11-12,45,62-69,128, 134
greens 52,53,56,84,123,134

H
harmonious colour 18-25
hot-pressed paper 27,28,29,76, 101,103,104,108

I
impact with colour 49,55,75,79,81

L
landscapes 70-97
Lawrence, Skip 11 -12,73,74-81
layering colours 41,55,56, 60-61,81, 83,103,121
over dried paint, 40,41,60
leaves 60,93-95,130,134
lifting colour 29,130,131
liquid acrylics 124-125
Lisiecki, Denise 17,34-41

M
masking agent 64,65,66,68
mauve 84,97
metallic colour 40,45
mixing with water 23,24,29,80, 104, 110, 111
moist paint 24-25,39
muted colour 75,108

N
non-staining watercolours 12-13,78, 81,118,122,134

O
objects with colour 34-41
opacity 24,27,36,61,76,79,81,95,131, 133

142   WATERCOLOUR PAINTING

P

painted colour washes 68
paper surface 20,27,28,36,48,56,64,76, 84,92,104,112,116,120
Pearse, Jeremy 101, 102-109,128
pointillist technique 96
poured colour washes 63,68
poured versus mixed colours 69
primary colour mixtures 117

R

raw sienna wash 88
reds 28,45,52,60,97,103,119,121, 123
related colours 26-33
relative value 73,80,88,128

S

scratching 117
sealing paint 58
shadows 40,41,61,66,87
sharpening edges 28,112,131
sky 96,131
softening edges 20,22,25,27,76,83,114,130
staining watercolours 13,24,63,66,81,91, 120,134
Stevens, Colleen Newport 101, 118-125
still lifes 14-41,65

T

thicker colour mixtures 25,83,115
thin washes 102-109
thinning paint 25
three-dimensional appearance 40
tonal washes 82-89
transparent colours 24,35,49,55,60,63, 64,76,84,92,119,121,122,133,134
trees 87, 88, 89,93-95
tube colours 13, 19, 24, 27, 32, 38,45, 52,53, 55, 56,60,63,68,134

U

underpainting 40,41,84

V

values 21,22,24,27,28,30, 36,41,57,65,73, 77,80,83,87,128,130
Van Campen, Susan Headley 45,46-53

W

Wade, Robert A. 73, 82-89
warm mixtures 109
watercolour dyes 124
Weilbaecher, Sharon 101, 110-117
Weinstein, Mary 45, 54-61, 134
wet-in-wet painting 83,85, 120, 131
wildlife 98-125
Wood, Robert E. 55

About the Author

M. STEPHEN DOHERTY is editor-in-chief of both *American Artist* and *Watercolor* magazines. He graduated summa cum laude and Phi Beta Kappa from Knox College in Galesburg, Illinois, and earned a master of fine arts degree in printmaking from Cornell University. He is the author of numerous magazine articles and books, including *Dynamic Still Lifes in Watercolor, Developing Ideas in Artwork, Business Letters for Artists, Creative Oil Painting* and *The Watson–Guptill Handbook of Landscape Painting*. Doherty frequently judges art competitions, offers lectures and critiques and exhibits his own paintings and prints. He is represented by the Bryant Galleries in New Orleans, Louisiana and Jackson, Mississippi.